D0468712

THE PASSIONS
AND THE
INTERESTS

Emblem No. 27 "Repress the Passions!" in Peter Iselburg,
Emblemata Politica, Nuremberg, 1617.

THE PASSIONS
AND THE
INTERESTS

*Political Arguments for Capitalism
before Its Triumph*

ALBERT O. HIRSCHMAN

PRINCETON UNIVERSITY PRESS
PRINCETON, NEW JERSEY

Copyright © 1977 by Princeton University Press

Published by Princeton University Press
Princeton, New Jersey
In the United Kingdom: Princeton University Press
Guildford, Surrey

Library of Congress Cataloging in Publication Data
will be found on the last printed page of this book

Publication of this book has been aided by the
Whitney Darrow Publication Reserve Fund
of Princeton University Press

Printed in the United States of America
by Princeton University Press
Princeton, New Jersey

Third printing, with corrections, 1981

Et il est heureux pour les hommes d'être dans une situation où, pendant que leurs passions leur inspirent la pensée d'être méchants, ils ont pourtant intérêt de ne pas l'être.

Montesquieu, *De l'esprit des lois*

ACKNOWLEDGMENTS

I WROTE a first draft of this book in 1972–73 while I was a visiting member at the Institute for Advanced Study, on sabbatical leave from Harvard University. In the course of the subsequent year, during which the manuscript had to be set aside, I was invited to join the Institute on a permanent basis and I accepted. Thereupon a substantial amount of rewriting and fattening up was accomplished in 1974–75 and only a quite limited further amount in 1975–76. I am very conscious that my argument could be considerably expanded, bolstered, qualified, bent, and adorned, but by March of this year I felt that it had reached a tolerable degree of closure and was anxious to expose my creation, errors and all, to the public. I am reminded of a Colombian Finance Minister in the fifties who was rather impulsive in issuing decrees and who explained to me, when I counseled prudence, that he did not have the funds needed to employ a large research staff: "If this decree really hurts some groups," so he would say, "they will do my research for me after the decree is out, and if they convince me I will issue another decree!" It is in this spirit that I am issuing my book, except that I cannot promise to any aggrieved parties or critics to write another one should I agree with them—but I doubt they would want me to.

Speaking of potential critics, I owe a special word of apology to J. G. A. Pocock whose *The Machiavellian Moment* (Princeton University Press, 1975) touches repeatedly on topics closely related to my own themes. Although I have greatly profited from a number of Professor Pocock's articles that were later incorporated into his monumental volume, the main arguments of my book had taken shape before I had a chance to read his. For this reason my treatment does not reflect as full an encounter with his point of view as would be desirable. Several people, none of whom are to be held responsible for the outcome, have helped me through advice or encouragement. The interchange of ideas and information among social scientists and historians at the Institute has been enormously useful; I profited particularly from conversations with David Bien and Pierre Bourdieu in 1972–73 and with Quentin Skinner and Donald Winch in 1974–75. The reactions of Judith Shklar and Michael Walzer to my first draft in 1973 were very important to me. Judith Tendler criticized this draft in considerable detail with her usual acumen. Finally, Sanford Thatcher of the Princeton University Press edited and otherwise processed the manuscript with remarkable competence, speed, and good spirits.

Princeton, New Jersey
May 1976

CONTENTS

Acknowledgments   vii

Introduction   3

PART ONE. How the Interests were Called
Upon to Counteract the Passions   7

    The Idea of Glory and Its Downfall   9

    Man "as he really is"   12

    Repressing and Harnessing the Passions   14

    The Principle of the Countervailing Passion   20

    "Interest" and "Interests" as Tamers of
      the Passions   31

    Interest as a New Paradigm   42

    Assets of an Interest-Governed World: Predictability
      and Constancy   48

    Money-Making and Commerce as Innocent
      and *Doux*   56

    Money-Making as a Calm Passion   63

PART TWO. How Economic Expansion was
Expected to Improve the Political Order   67

    Elements of a Doctrine   70

      1. Montesquieu   70

      2. Sir James Steuart   81

      3. John Millar   87

    Related yet Discordant Views   93

      1. The Physiocrats   96

      2. Adam Smith and the End of a Vision   100

CONTENTS

PART THREE. Reflections on an Episode in
Intellectual History   115

    Where the Montesquieu-Steuart Vision Went
      Wrong   117

    The Promise of an Interest-Governed World
      versus the Protestant Ethic   128

    Contemporary Notes   132

Notes   136

Index   146

THE PASSIONS
AND THE
INTERESTS

INTRODUCTION

THIS essay has its origin in the incapacity of contemporary social science to shed light on the political consequences of economic growth and, perhaps even more, in the so frequently calamitous political correlates of economic growth no matter whether such growth takes place under capitalist, socialist, or mixed auspices. Reasoning about such connections, I suspected, must have been rife at an earlier age of economic expansion, specifically the seventeenth and eighteenth centuries. With the "disciplines" of economics and political science not yet in existence at the time, there were no interdisciplinary boundaries to cross. As a result, philosophers and political economists could range freely and speculate without inhibitions about the likely consequences of, say, commercial expansion for peace, or of industrial growth for liberty. It seemed worthwhile to look back at their thoughts and speculations, if only because of our own, specialization-induced intellectual poverty in this field.

Such was the original motivation of the present essay, the idea that prompted me to venture into the edifice of seventeenth- and eighteenth-century social thought. Given the rich and complex nature of this edifice, it is not surprising that I emerged with something rather broader and even more ambitious than what I had come to look for. In fact, the very answers to the questions I began with yielded, as an intriguing by-product, a new approach to the interpretation of the "spirit" of capitalism and of its emergence. It may be useful here to outline this approach, reserving a fuller presentation for the last part of this study.

A vast literature has contrasted the aristocratic, heroic ideal of the Feudal Age and the Renaissance with the bourgeois mentality and the Protestant Ethic of a later era. The decline of one ethic and the rise of another have been exhaustively surveyed and have been presented as precisely such: as two distinct historical processes, each of which had as its protagonist a different social class, the declining aristocracy on the one hand, and the rising bourgeoisie on the other. Historians have of course found it attractive to present the story as a pageant in the course of which a young challenger takes on the aging champion. But this conception has appealed equally, if not more, to those searching for scientific knowledge of society and its so-called laws of motion. While the Marxian and Weberian analyses disagree on the relative importance of economic and noneconomic factors, they both view the rise of capitalism and of its "spirit" as an assault on preexisting systems of ideas and of socioeconomic relations.

A group of historians has recently questioned the class character of the French Revolution. In dealing here with the history of ideas I do not aspire to be quite so iconoclastic; but, in a similar vein, I shall present some evidence that the new arose out of the old to a greater extent than has generally been appreciated. To portray a lengthy ideological change or transition as an endogenous process is of course more complex than to depict it as the rise of an independently conceived, insurgent ideology concurrent with the decline of a hitherto dominant ethic. A portrayal of this sort involves the identification of a sequence of concatenated ideas and propositions whose final outcome is necessarily hidden from the proponents of the individual links, at least in the early stages of the process; for they would have shuddered—and revised their thinking—had they realized where their ideas would ultimately lead.

In the reconstruction of such a sequence of linked ideas one must normally draw on evidence from many sources and can give but scant attention to the systems of thought in which that evidence is embedded. This is indeed the procedure followed in the first part of this essay. In the second part the focus narrows to concentrate on the high points of the sequence. The authors who have fully developed these points, such as Montesquieu and Sir James Steuart, are treated at greater length, and an effort is made to understand how the specific propositions underlined for the purposes of our story relate to their general way of thinking. The third part of the essay comments on the historical significance of the intellectual episode here presented and on its relevance for some of our contemporary predicaments.

PART ONE

How the Interests were Called Upon
to Counteract the Passions

The Idea of Glory and Its Downfall

A T THE beginning of the principal section of his famous essay, Max Weber asked: "Now, how could an activity, which was at best ethically tolerated, turn into a calling in the sense of Benjamin Franklin?"[1] In other words: How did commercial, banking, and similar money-making pursuits become honorable at some point in the modern age after having stood condemned or despised as greed, love of lucre, and avarice for centuries past?

The enormous critical literature on *The Protestant Ethic* has found fault even with this point of departure of Weber's inquiry. The "spirit of capitalism," it has been alleged, was extant among merchants as far back as the fourteenth and fifteenth centuries, and a positive attitude toward certain categories of business pursuits could be discovered in the writings of the Scholastics.[2]

Weber's question is nevertheless justified if it is asked in a comparative vein. No matter how much approval was bestowed on commerce and other forms of money-making, they certainly stood lower in the scale of medieval values than a number of other activities, in particular the striving for glory. It is indeed through a brief sketch of the idea of glory in the Middle Ages and the Renaissance that I shall now attempt to renew the sense of wonder about the genesis of the "spirit of capitalism."

At the beginning of the Christian era St. Augustine had supplied basic guidelines to medieval thinking by denouncing lust for money and possessions as one of the three principal sins of fallen man, lust for power (*libido dominandi*) and sexual lust being the other two.[3] On

9

the whole Augustine is perfectly even-handed in his condemnation of these three human drives or passions. If he does admit of attenuating circumstances for any of them, it is for *libido dominandi* when combined with a strong desire for praise and glory. Thus Augustine speaks of the "civil virtue" characterizing the early Romans "who have shown a Babylonian love for their earthly fatherland," and who were "suppressing the desire of wealth and many other vices for their one vice, namely, the love of praise."[4]

For the later argument of this essay it is of considerable interest that St. Augustine conceives here of the possibility that one vice may check another. In any event, his limited endorsement of glory-seeking left an opening that was broadened far beyond his teachings by the spokesmen for the chivalric, aristocratic ideal who made the striving for honor and glory into the touchstone of a man's virtue and greatness. What Augustine had expressed most cautiously and reluctantly was later triumphantly proclaimed: love of glory, in contrast with the purely private pursuit of riches, can have "redeeming social value." In fact, the idea of an "Invisible Hand"—of a force that makes men pursuing their private passions conspire unknowingly toward the public good—was formulated in connection with the search for glory, rather than with the desire for money, by Montesquieu. The pursuit of honor in a monarchy, so he says, "brings life to all the parts of the body politic"; as a result, "it turns out that everyone contributes to the general welfare while thinking that he works for his own interests."[5]

With or without such sophisticated justification, striving for honor and glory was exalted by the medieval chivalric ethos even though it stood at odds with the central teachings, not only of St. Augustine, but of a long line of religious writers, from St. Thomas Aquinas to Dante, who attacked glory-seeking as both vain *(inanis)* and sinful.[6] Then, during the Renaissance, the striving for honor achieved the status of a dominant ideology as the influence of the Church receded and the advocates of the aristocratic ideal were able to draw on the plentiful Greek and Roman texts celebrating the pursuit of glory.[7] This powerful intellectual current carried over into the seventeenth century: perhaps the purest conception of glory-seeking as the only justification of life is to be found in the tragedies of Corneille. At the same time, Corneille's formulations were so extreme that they may have contributed to the spectacular downfall of the aristocratic ideal that was to be staged by some of his contemporaries.[8]

Writers from a number of Western European countries cooperated in this "demolition of the hero,"[9] with those from France—the country that had perhaps gone farthest in the cult of the heroic ideal—playing the major part. All the heroic virtues were shown to be forms of mere self-preservation by Hobbes, of self-love by La Rochefoucauld, of vanity and of frantic escape from real self-knowledge by Pascal. The heroic passions were portrayed as demeaning by Racine after having been denounced as foolish, if not demented, by Cervantes.

This astounding transformation of the moral and ideological scene erupts quite suddenly, and the historical and psychological reasons for it are still not wholly understood. The principal point to be made here is that those responsible for the demolition did not downgrade the traditional values in order to propound a new moral code that might have corresponded to the interests or

11

needs of a new class. Denunciation of the heroic ideal
was nowhere associated with the advocacy of a new bourgeois ethos. Obvious as this statement is with respect to
Pascal and La Rochefoucauld, it also holds for Hobbes,
some interpretations to the contrary notwithstanding.[10]
For a long time it was thought that Molière's plays had
as their message the praise of bourgeois virtues, but once
again this interpretation has been shown to be unten-
able.[11]

By itself, therefore, the demolition of the heroic ideal
could have only restored the equality in ignominy that
Augustine had meant to bestow on love of money and
lust for power and glory (not to mention lust proper).
The fact is of course that, less than a century later, the
acquisitive drive and the activities connected with it,
such as commerce, banking, and eventually industry,
came to be widely hailed, for a variety of reasons. But
this enormous change did not result from any simple
victory of one fully armed ideology over another. The
real story is far more complex and roundabout.

Man "as he really is"

THE beginning of that story does come with the Renaissance, but not through the development of a new
ethic, that is, of new rules of conduct for the *individual*.
Rather, it will be traced here to a new turn in the theory
of the *state*, to the attempt at improving statecraft
within the existing order. To insist on this point of
departure proceeds of course from the endogenous bias
of the tale I propose to tell.

In attempting to teach the prince how to achieve,

maintain, and expand power, Machiavelli made his fundamental and celebrated distinction between "the effective truth of things" and the "imaginary republics and monarchies that have never been seen nor have been known to exist."[12] The implication was that moral and political philosophers had hitherto talked exclusively about the latter and had failed to provide guidance to the real world in which the prince must operate. This demand for a scientific, positive approach was extended only later from the prince to the individual, from the nature of the state to human nature. Machiavelli probably sensed that a realistic theory of the state required a knowledge of human nature, but his remarks on that subject, while invariably acute, are scattered and unsystematic. By the next century a considerable change had occurred. The advances of mathematics and celestial mechanics held out the hope that laws of motion might be discovered for men's actions, just as for falling bodies and planets. Thus Hobbes, who based his theory of human nature on Galileo,[13] devotes the first ten chapters of *Leviathan* to the nature of man before proceeding to that of the commonwealth. But it was Spinoza who reiterated, with particular sharpness and vehemence,[a] Machiavelli's charges against the utopian thinkers of the past, this time in relation to individual human behavior. In the opening paragraph of the *Tractatus politicus* he attacks the philosophers who "conceive men not as they are but as they would like them to be." And this distinction between positive and normative

[a] Leo Strauss in *Spinoza's Critique of Religion* (New York: Schocken, 1965), p. 277, notes "the striking fact that Spinoza's tone is much sharper than that of Machiavelli." He attributes this to the fact that, being primarily a philosopher, Spinoza was personally much more involved with utopian thought than Machiavelli, the political scientist.

thinking appears again in the *Ethics,* where Spinoza opposes to those who "prefer to detest and scoff at human affects and actions" his own famous project to "consider human actions and appetites just as if I were considering lines, planes, or bodies."[14]

That man "as he really is" is the proper subject of what is today called political science continued to be asserted—sometimes almost routinely—in the eighteenth century. Vico, who had read Spinoza, followed him faithfully in this respect, if not in others. He writes in the *Scienza nuova:*

> Philosophy considers man as he ought to be and is therefore useful only to the very few who want to live in Plato's Republic and do not throw themselves into the dregs of Romulus. Legislation considers man as he is and attempts to put him to good uses in human society.[15]

Even Rousseau, whose view of human nature was far removed from those of Machiavelli and Hobbes, pays tribute to the idea by opening the *Contrat social* with the sentence: "Taking men as they are and the laws as they might be, I wish to investigate whether a legitimate and certain principle of government can be encountered."

Repressing and Harnessing the Passions

THE overwhelming insistence on looking at man "as he really is" has a simple explanation. A feeling arose in the Renaissance and became firm conviction during the seventeenth century that moralizing philosophy and religious precept could no longer be trusted with restraining the destructive passions of men. New ways had to be found and the search for them began quite logically with a detailed and candid dissection of human nature. There were those like La Rochefoucauld who delved into its recesses and proclaimed their "savage discoveries" with so much gusto that the dissection looks very much like an end in itself. But in general it was undertaken to discover more effective ways of shaping the pattern of human actions than through moralistic exhortation or the threat of damnation. And, naturally enough, the search was successful; in fact, one can distinguish between at least three lines of argument that were proposed as alternatives to the reliance on religious command.

The most obvious alternative, which actually antedates the movement of ideas here surveyed, is the appeal to coercion and repression. The task of holding back, by force if necessary, the worst manifestations and the most dangerous consequences of the passions is entrusted to the state. This was the thought of St. Augustine, which was to be closely echoed in the sixteenth century by Calvin.[16] Any established social and political order is justified by its very existence. Its possible injustices are just retributions for the sins of Fallen Man.

The political systems of St. Augustine and Calvin are in some respects closely related to that advocated in *Leviathan*. But the crucial invention of Hobbes is his peculiar transactional concept of the Covenant, which is quite alien in spirit to those earlier authoritarian systems. Notoriously difficult to pigeonhole, the thought of Hobbes will be discussed under a different category.

The repressive solution to the problem posed by the recognition of man's unruly passions has great difficulties. For what if the sovereign fails to do his job properly, because of excessive leniency, cruelty, or some other failing? Once this question is asked, the prospect of the establishment of an appropriately repressive sovereign or authority appears to be of the same order of probability as the prospect that men will restrain their passions because of the exhortations of moralizing philosophers or churchmen. As the latter prospect is held to be nil, the repressive solution turns out to be in contradiction with its own premises. To imagine an authority *ex machina* that would somehow suppress the misery and havoc men inflict on each other as a result of their passions means in effect to wish away, rather than to solve, the very difficulties that have been discovered. It is perhaps for this reason that the repressive solution did not long survive the detailed analysis of the passions in the seventeenth century.

A solution that is more in harmony with these psychological discoveries and preoccupations consists in the idea of *harnessing* the passions, instead of simply repressing them. Once again the state, or "society," is called upon to perform this feat, yet this time not merely as a repressive bulwark, but as a transformer, a civilizing medium. Speculations about such a transformation of the disruptive passions into something constructive can be encountered already in the seventeenth century. Anticipating Adam Smith's Invisible Hand, Pascal argues for man's grandeur on the ground that he "has managed to tease out of concupiscence an admirable arrangement" and "so beautiful an order."[b]

[b] *Pensées*, Nos. 402, 403 (Brunschvicg edn.). The idea that a society held together by self-love rather than by charity can be workable in spite of being sinful is found among a number of prominent Jansenist contemporaries of Pascal, such as Nicole and

In the early eighteenth century Giambattista Vico articulated the idea more fully while characteristically endowing it with the flavor of an exciting discovery:

> Out of ferocity, avarice, and ambition, the three vices which lead all mankind astray, [society] makes national defense, commerce, and politics, and thereby causes the strength, the wealth, and the wisdom of the republics; out of these three great vices which would certainly destroy man on earth, society thus causes the civil happiness to emerge. This principle proves the existence of divine providence: through its intelligent laws the passions of men who are entirely occupied by the pursuit of their private utility are transformed into a civil order which permits men to live in human society.[17]

This is clearly one of those statements to which Vico owes his fame as an extraordinarily seminal mind. Hegel's Cunning of Reason, the Freudian concept of sublimation and, once again, Adam Smith's Invisible Hand can all be read into these two pregnant sentences. But there is no elaboration and we are left in the dark about the conditions under which that marvelous metamorphosis of destructive "passions" into "virtues" actually takes place.

The idea of harnessing the passions of men, of making them work toward the general welfare, was put forward at considerably greater length by Vico's English con-

---

Domat. See Gilbert Chinard, *En lisant Pascal* (Lille: Giarel, 1948), pp. 97–118, and D. W. Smith, *Helvetius: A Study in Persecution* (Oxford: Clarendon Press, 1965), pp. 122–125. A fine recent study of Nicole is in Nannerl O. Keohane, "Non-Conformist Absolutism in Louis XIV's France: Pierre Nicole and Denis Veiras," *Journal of the History of Ideas* 35 (Oct.-Dec. 1974), pp. 579–596.

temporary, Bernard Mandeville. Often regarded as a precursor of laissez-faire, Mandeville actually invoked throughout *The Fable of the Bees* the "Skilful Management of the Dextrous Politician" as a necessary condition and agent for the turning of "private vices" into "publick benefits." Since the modus operandi of the Politician was not revealed, however, there remained considerable mystery about the alleged beneficial and paradoxical transformations. Only for one specific "private vice" did Mandeville supply a detailed demonstration of how such transformations are in fact accomplished. I am referring, of course, to his celebrated treatment of the passion for material goods in general, and for luxury in particular.[c]

It may therefore be said that Mandeville restricted the area in which he effectively claimed validity for his paradox to one particular "vice" or passion. In this retreat from generality he was to be followed, with the well-known resounding success, by the Adam Smith of *The Wealth of Nations,* a work that was wholly focused on the passion traditionally known as cupidity or avarice. Moreover, because of the intervening evolution of language, to be considered at some length later in this essay, Smith was able to take a further giant step in the direction of making the proposition palatable and per-

[c] It has been convincingly argued that by "Dextrous Management" Mandeville did not mean detailed day-to-day intervention and regulation but rather the slow elaboration and evolution, by trial and error, of an appropriate legal and institutional framework. See Nathan Rosenberg, "Mandeville and Laissez-Faire," *Journal of the History of Ideas* 24 (April-June 1963), pp. 183–196. But, again, the modus operandi of this framework is assumed rather than demonstrated by Mandeville. And regarding luxury, whose favorable effects on the general welfare he does describe in detail, the active roles of the Politician or of the institutional framework are not at all prominent.

suasive: he blunted the edge of Mandeville's shocking paradox by substituting for "passion" and "vice" such bland terms as "advantage" or "interest."

In this limited and domesticated form the harnessing idea was able to survive and to prosper both as a major tenet of nineteenth-century liberalism and as a central construct of economic theory. But retreat from the generality of the harnessing idea was far from universal. In fact, some of its later adepts were even less careful than Vico: for them the onward march of history was proof enough that somehow the passions of men conspire to the general progress of mankind or of the World Spirit. Herder and Hegel both wrote along such lines in their works on the philosophy of history.[d] Hegel's famous concept of the Cunning of Reason expresses the idea that men, following their passions, actually serve some higher world-historical purpose of which they are totally unaware. It is perhaps significant that the concept does not reappear in Hegel's *Philosophy of Law* where he is concerned, not with the sweep of world history, but with the actual evolution of society in his own time. So blanket an endorsement of the passions as is implicit in the Cunning of Reason obviously had no place in any work that took a critical view of contemporary social and political development.

A final representative of the idea at its most unguarded is the Mephisto of Goethe's *Faust* with his famous self-definition as "a portion of that force that always wills evil and always brings forth good." Here it

[d] According to Herder, "all passions of man's breast are wild drives of a force which does not know itself yet, but which, in accordance with its nature, can only conspire toward a better order of things." *Ideen zur Philosophie der Geschichte der Menschheit* in *Werke*, ed. Suphan (Berlin, 1909), Vol. 14, p. 215.

seems that the idea of harnessing the evil passions in some concrete manner has been abandoned altogether— instead, their transformation is accomplished through an occult, if beneficent, world process.

The Principle of the Countervailing Passion

GIVEN the overwhelming reality of restless, passion- ate, driven man, both the repressive and the har- nessing solutions lacked persuasiveness. The repressive solution was a manner of assuming the problem away, whereas the greater realism of the harnessing solution was marred by an element of alchemical transformation rather out of tune with the scientific enthusiasm of the age.

The very material with which the moralists of the seventeenth century were dealing—the detailed descrip- tion and investigation of the passions—was bound to suggest a third solution: Is it not possible to discriminate among the passions and fight fire with fire—to utilize one set of comparatively innocuous passions to counter- vail another more dangerous and destructive set or, per- haps, to weaken and tame the passions by such inter- necine fights in *divide et impera* fashion? It seems a simple and obvious thought once one despairs of the efficacy of moralizing yet, in spite of St. Augustine's passing hint, it was probably a more difficult one to come up with than the project of attacking all the passions simultaneously. The major passions had long been sol- idly linked to one another in literature and thought, often in some unholy trinity, from Dante's "Superbia, invidia e avarizia sono / le tre faville ch'anno i cuori

COUNTERACTING THE PASSIONS

accesi"[e] to "Ehrsucht, Herrschsucht und Habsucht"[f] in Kant's *Idea for a General History*. Much like the three scourges of mankind—war, famine, pestilence—these basic passions were believed to feed on each other. The habit of considering them as indissoluble was further reinforced by their being ordinarily contrasted as a bloc with the dictates of reason or the requirements of salvation.

Medieval allegories had frequently depicted just such fights of the virtues against the vices, with the soul of man as battleground.[g] Perhaps it was paradoxically this tradition that made it possible for a later, more realistic age to conceive of a very different kind of fight, which would pit one passion against another, while still redounding, just as the earlier one, to the benefit of man and mankind. In any event, the idea arose and did so in fact at opposite ends of the thought and personality spectrum of the seventeenth century: Bacon and Spinoza.

For Bacon, the idea was a consequence of his systematic attempt at shaking off the metaphysical and theological yokes that kept men from thinking inductively and experimentally. In the sections of *The Advancement of Learning* that deal with the "Appetite and Will of Man" he criticizes traditional moral philosophers for having acted

[e] Pride, envy, and greed are the three sparks that set men's hearts afire. *Inferno*, Canto VI, lines 74–75.

[f] Ambition, lust for power, and greed.

[g] For this reason the genre is known as psychomachy. Its history, from the *Psychomachia* of Prudentius, a fifth-century work, to the virtue and vice cycle on the central porch of the façade of Notre-Dame-de-Paris, is traced in Adolf Katzenellenbogen, *Allegories of the Virtues and Vices in Mediaeval Art* (London: Warburg Institute, 1939).

as if a man that professeth to teach to write did
only exhibit fair copies of alphabets and letters
joined, without giving any precepts or directions
for the carriage of the hand and framing of the letters. So have they made good and fair examples and
copies, carrying the draughts of Good, Virtue, Duty,
Felicity; . . . but how to attain these excellent
marks, and how to frame and subdue the will of
man to become true and conformable to these pursuits, they pass it over altogether. . . .[18]

Although the critique is familiar since Machiavelli, the
simile is remarkably suggestive and a few pages later
Bacon tries his own hand at the task he has outlined.
He does so in the guise of commending poets and historians—in contrast to philosophers—for having

painted forth with great life, how affections are
kindled and incited; how pacified and refrained;
. . . how they disclose themselves, how they work,
how they vary, how they gather and fortify, how
they are inwrapped one within another, and how
they do fight and encounter one with another, and
other the like particularities; amongst which this
last is of special use in moral and civil matters;
*how (I say) to set affection against affection and to
master one by another*: even as we use to hunt beast
with beast and fly bird with bird. . . . For as in the
government of states it is sometimes necessary to
bridle one faction with another, so it is in the government within.[19]

This forceful paragraph, particularly its latter part,
has all the earmarks of being based, not so much on the
accomplishments of poets and historians, as on Bacon's

own intensive personal experience as a politician and statesman. The idea of controlling the passions by playing one off against the other is, moreover, highly congruent with the irreverent and experimental bent of his thought. On the other hand, his formulation does not seem to have been particularly influential at the time. Only modern scholarship has called attention to it in order to present Bacon in this respect as a forerunner of Spinoza and Hume, who gave the idea a far more central place in their systems.[20]

In elaborating his theory of the passions in the *Ethics*, Spinoza puts forth two propositions that are essential for the development of his argument:

> An affect cannot be restrained nor removed unless by an opposed and stronger affect.[21]

and

> No affect can be restrained by the true knowledge of good and evil insofar as it is true, but only insofar as it is considered as an affect.[22]

At first sight it seems strange that Spinoza, with his metaphysical bent and his comparative lack of involvement in the life of action, should have espoused the same doctrine as Bacon. He did so in fact for quite different reasons. Nothing could have been farther from his mind than the thought that the passions could be usefully restrained and manipulated by setting one passion against the other. The passages just quoted served primarily to emphasize the strength and autonomy of the passions so that the real difficulties of attaining the final destination of Spinoza's journey in the *Ethics* would be fully realized. That destination is the triumph of reason and love of God over the passions, and the idea of the countervailing passion functions as a mere way station leading to it. At the same time, the idea remains an integral part of the culmination of Spinoza's work, as is evident from its very last proposition:

> . . . [we do not] delight in blessedness because we restrain our lusts; but, on the contrary, because we delight in it, therefore we are able to restrain them.[23]

The first great philosopher who gave pride of place to the idea that passions can be fought successfully only through other passions had therefore no intention whatever of translating this idea into the realm of practical moral or political engineering, even though he had a lively appreciation of such possibilities.[h] Indeed, the thought does not recur in Spinoza's political works, which otherwise do not lack in practical suggestions on how to make the quirks of human nature work out to the advantage of society.

Although Hume denounced Spinoza's philosophy as "hideous," his ideas on the passions and their relation to reason are remarkably close to Spinoza's.[24] Hume was simply more radical in proclaiming the imperviousness of the passions to reason; "reason is, and ought only to be the slave of the passions" is one of his best known pronouncements. In view of this extreme position he was badly in need of the consoling thought that one passion can function as the counterpoise to another. He proclaims it indeed in the same crucial paragraph: "Noth-

[h] As is shown, for example, by the following sentence: "By contrary affects, I understand in the following pages those which, although they may be of the same kind, draw a man in different directions; such as voluptuousness and avarice, which are both a species of love. . . ." *Ethics*, Part IV, Definitions.

ing can oppose or retard the impulse of passion but a contrary impulse."[25]

Unlike Spinoza, Hume was eager to apply his insight. He did so immediately in Book III of the *Treatise* when discussing the "origin of society." Speaking of the "avidity . . . of acquiring goods and possessions," he finds this so potentially destructive and also so uniquely powerful a passion that the only way of checking it is to have it *countervail itself*. This does not seem an easy operation to perform, but here is how Hume solves the problem:

> There is no passion, therefore, capable of controlling the interested affection, but the very affection itself, by an alteration of its direction. Now this alteration must necessarily take place upon the least reflection; since 'tis evident, that the passion is much better satisfy'd by its restraint, than by its liberty, and that in preserving society, we make much greater advances in the acquiring of possessions, than in the solitary and forlorn condition. . . .[26]

One might of course quibble that to avow the need for some reason or reflection, however "least," means to introduce an alien element (which, moreover, is supposed to be the "slave of the passions") into an arena in which only passion is supposed to fight with passion. The point here, however, is not to note flaws in Hume's thought but to demonstrate the hold that the idea of the countervailing passion had on him. He uses it more felicitously in a number of less momentous applications. In discussing Mandeville, for example, he argues that although luxury is an evil, it may be a lesser evil than "sloth," which might result from banishing luxury:

Let us, therefore, rest contented with asserting that two opposite vices in a state may be more advantageous than either of them alone; but let us never pronounce vice in itself advantageous.

A more general formulation follows:

Whatever may be the consequence of such a miraculous transformation of mankind as would endow them with every species of virtue, and free them from every species of vice; this concerns not the magistrate who aims only at possibilities. Very often he can only cure one vice by another; and in that case, he ought to prefer what is least pernicious to society.[27]

Elsewhere, as will be noted below, Hume advocated restraining the "love of pleasure" by the "love of gain." And other applications of the idea obviously fascinated him even when he did not agree, as in the following passage, taken from the essay on "The Sceptic":

"Nothing can be more destructive," says Fontenelle, "to ambition and the passion for conquest, than the true system of astronomy. What a poor thing is even the whole globe in comparison [to] the infinite extent of nature?" This consideration is evidently too distant ever to have any effect. Or, if it had any, would it not destroy patriotism as well as ambition?[28]

This polemic suggests that the idea of engineering social progress by cleverly setting up one passion to fight another became a fairly common intellectual pastime in the course of the eighteenth century. It is indeed expressed by a host of writers, minor as well as major, in general or applied form. The latter genre is illustrated by the article on "Fanaticism" in the *Encyclopédie*; essentially a spirited diatribe against religious institutions and beliefs, it ends with a special section on "the fanaticism of the patriot," which is praised largely because it can usefully counteract religious fanaticism.[29] By contrast, the idea is conveyed in its most general form by Vauvenargues:

> Passions are opposed to passions and one can serve as a counterweight to another.[30]

And the same language is found in the more elaborate formulation of d'Holbach:

> The passions are the true counterweights of the passions; we must not at all attempt to destroy them, but rather try to direct them: let us offset those that are harmful by those that are useful to society. Reason . . . is nothing but the act of choosing those passions which we must follow for the sake of our happiness.[31]

The principle of the countervailing passion had arisen in the seventeenth century on the basis of its somber view of human nature and of a general belief that the passions are dangerous and destructive. In the course of the succeeding century both human nature and the passions came to be widely rehabilitated.[i] In France the boldest defender of the passions was Helvétius.[32] His position is sufficiently indicated by such chapter headings from *De l'esprit* as "On the power of the passions," "On the intellectual superiority of passionate over sensible people *(gens sensés)*," and "One becomes stupid as soon as one ceases to be passionate." But just as Rousseau repeated routinely the call for looking at man "as

[i] See also below, p. 64.

he really is" even though his concept of human nature was totally different from that which was responsible for the call having been issued in the first place, so the countervailing-passion remedy continued to be advocated even though the passions were now pronounced to be invigorating rather than pernicious. In fact, Helvétius produced one of the finest statements of the principle, one that harks right back to Bacon's original formula with, to be sure, a dash of rococo added:

> There are few moralists who know how to arm our passions against one another . . . for the purpose of having their counsel adopted. Most of the time their advice is too injurious. Yet they should realize that this sort of injurious discourse cannot win out over feeling; that only a passion can triumph over a passion; that, for example, if one wishes to induce more modesty and restraint in a forward woman (*femme galante*) one ought to set her vanity against her coquetry and make her realize that modesty is an invention of love and of refined voluptuousness. . . . The moralists might succeed in having their maxims observed *if they replaced in this manner their injurious discourse by the language of interest.*[33]

For the next step in our argument, it is particularly significant that the word "interest" was here used as a generic term for those passions that are assigned the countervailing function.

From France and England the idea traveled to America where it was used by the Founding Fathers as an important intellectual tool for the purposes of constitutional engineering.[34] A fine—and, in view of recent experience with the Presidency, highly topical—example is in Number 72 of *The Federalist*, where Hamilton justifies the principle of reelection for the President. His argument runs largely in terms of what prohibition of reelection would do to the incumbent's motivations. Among other ill effects, he says, there would be the "temptation to sordid views, to peculation":

> An avaricious man, who might happen to fill the office, looking forward to the time when he must at all events yield up the emoluments he enjoyed, would feel a propensity, not easy to be resisted by such a man, to make the best use of the opportunity he enjoyed while it lasted, and might not scruple to have recourse to the most corrupt expedients to make the harvest as abundant as it was transitory; though the same man, probably, with a different prospect before him, might content himself with the regular perquisites of his situation, and might even be unwilling to risk the consequences of an abuse of his opportunities. His avarice might be a guard upon his avarice. Add to this that the same man might be vain or ambitious, as well as avaricious. And if he could expect to prolong his honours by his good conduct, he might hesitate to sacrifice his appetite for them to his appetite for gain. But with the prospect before him of approaching an inevitable annihilation, his avarice would be likely to get the victory over his caution, his vanity, or his ambition.

The last sentences show real virtuosity in the handling of the countervailing idea, so much so that they leave the modern reader, rather less well trained along these lines, a bit breathless.

A better known instance of reasoning that *seems* very

similar is in *Federalist* 51, where the division of powers among the various branches of government is eloquently justified by the statement that "ambition must be made to counteract ambition." The meaning here is that the ambition of one branch of government is expected to counter that of another, a situation very different from the previous one in which the passions are seen to be fighting it out within the arena of a *single* soul. But it may be significant that the principle of the division of powers was given the attire of another: the comparatively novel thought of checks and balances gained in persuasiveness by being presented as an application of the widely accepted and thoroughly familiar principle of countervailing passion.

It was not a conscious stratagem of course. In fact, the author of that sentence (Hamilton or Madison) appears to have become the first victim of the confusion it fostered, for he continues: "It may be a reflection on human nature that such devices should be necessary to control the abuses of government. But what is government itself but the greatest of all reflections on human nature?" Now it certainly is a "reflection on human nature" to hold that man's evil impulses can only be restrained by setting up his various passions to fight and neutralize each other. The principle of the division of powers, on the other hand, is not nearly so insulting to human nature. It looks therefore as though by writing the lapidary sentence "ambition must be made to counteract ambition" its author persuaded himself that the principle of countervailing passion, rather than that of checks and balances, was the foundation of the new state.

Speaking more generally, it seems rather plausible that the former principle laid the intellectual groundwork for the principle of separation of powers. In this manner the train of thought studied here returned to its point of departure: it had started with the state, whence it turned to consider problems of individual conduct, and in due course the insights yielded by this phase were imported back into the theory of politics.

"Interest" and "Interests" as Tamers of the Passions

ONCE the strategy of pitting passion against passion had been devised and was considered acceptable and even promising, a further step in the sequence of reasoning here described became desirable: for the strategy to have ready applicability, to become "operational" in today's jargon, one ought to know, at least in a general way, which passions were typically to be assigned the role of tamers and which ones, on the contrary, were the truly "wild" passions that required taming.

A specific role assignment of this sort underlies the Hobbesian Covenant, which is concluded only because the "Desires, and other Passions of men," such as the aggressive pursuit of riches, glory, and dominion, are overcome by those other "passions that incline men to Peace," which are "Feare of Death; Desire of such things as are necessary to commodious living; and a Hope by their Industry to obtain them."[35] The whole of the social contract doctrine is, in this sense, an offshoot of the countervailing strategy. Hobbes needs to appeal to it just *once*, for the purpose of *founding* a state so constituted that the problems created by passionate men are solved once and for all. With this task in mind it was sufficient for him to define the taming and to-be-tamed passions on an ad hoc basis. But many contemporaries of Hobbes, while sharing his concern about the predicament of man and society, did not embrace his radical solution and felt, moreover, that the countervailing strategy was needed on a continuing, day-to-day basis. For this purpose a more general and permanent formulation of the role assignment was clearly desirable. Such a formulation emerged in fact and took the form of opposing the *interests* of men to their *passions* and of contrasting the favorable effects that follow when men are guided by their interests with the calamitous state of affairs that prevails when men give free rein to their passions.

To understand the opposition of these two concepts, something must first be said about the various successive (and often simultaneous) meanings of the terms "interest" and "interests" in the course of the evolution of language and ideas. "Interests" of persons and groups eventually came to be centered on economic advantage as its core meaning, not only in ordinary language but also in such social-science terms as "class interests" and "interest groups." But the economic meaning became dominant rather late in the history of the term. When the term "interest" in the sense of concerns, aspirations, and advantage gained currency in Western Europe during the late sixteenth century, its meaning was by no means limited to the material aspects of a person's welfare; rather, it comprised the totality of human aspirations, but denoted an element of reflection and calculation with respect to the manner in which these aspirations were to be pursued.[j] In fact, serious thought

[j] The history of the term goes back much farther for its other meanings, such as the interest that is charged on borrowed money and the strange French usage in which *intérêt* meant injury and loss—a meaning still evident in the contemporary *dommages-intérêts*.

involving the notion of interest first arose in a context entirely removed from individuals and their material welfare. Earlier it was shown how concern for improving the quality of statecraft was at the origins of the quest for greater realism in the analysis of human behavior. This same concern led to the first definition and detailed investigation of "interest."

Once again Machiavelli stands at the source of the flow of ideas to be examined, just as he had initiated the train of thought that developed into the notion of pitting passions against passions. As we shall see, these two flows ran separately for a long time, but in the end they merged—with some remarkable results.

Machiavelli actually did not name his child. He prescribed a characteristic behavior for rulers of states, but did not subsume it under a single expression. Later his works did inspire the twin, initially synonymous terms *interesse* and *ragione di stato*, which came into widespread use in the second half of the sixteenth century, as shown in Meinecke's great study.[36] These concepts were meant to do battle on two fronts: on the one hand, they were obviously a declaration of independence from the moralizing precepts and rules that had been the mainstay of pre-Machiavellian political philosophy; but, at the same time, they aimed at identifying a "sophisticated, rational will, untroubled by passions and momentary impulses,"[37] that would give clear and sound guidance to the prince.

The main battle of Machiavelli, the founder of the new statecraft, was of course waged on the first front, even though Meinecke shows that he was by no means oblivious of the second.[38] The *constraints* that the concept of interest as guidepost for action implied for the rulers came to the fore as it travelled from Italy to

France and England. They stand out sharply in the famous opening sentence of the essay *On the Interest of Princes and States of Christendom* (1638) by the Huguenot statesman, the Duke of Rohan:

> Les princes commandent aux peuples, et l'intérêt commande aux princes.[k]

As Meinecke points out, Rohan may have borrowed this formulation from such earlier Italian writers on statecraft as Boccalini and Bonaventura, who had called interest the "tyrant of tyrants" and *ragione di stato* the "prince of the prince."[39] But Rohan goes to considerable length to drive his point home. Having outlined in general terms the national interests of Spain, France, Italy, England, and the other principal powers of his time, he proceeds, in the second part of his essay, to recount some historical episodes intended to show that

> in matters of state one must not let oneself be guided by disorderly appetites, which make us often undertake tasks beyond our strength; nor by violent passions, which agitate us in various ways as soon as they possess us; . . . but by our own interest guided by reason alone, which must be the rule of our actions.[l]

And, indeed, this programmatic pronouncement is followed by several examples of princes who have come to grief because they followed their passions rather than their interest.

It is richly ironical that the new doctrine of princely

---

[k] Princes order their people around and interest orders princes around.

[l] Introduction to Part II. Significantly, reason is here downgraded to the purely instrumental role of figuring out where the true interest of the state lies.

interest should have come to warn and inveigh against indulging the passions so soon after the moralizing and religious precepts of old had been ridiculed as unrealistic and useless. This irony was not lost on the purveyors of these precepts, and some of them were happy enough to take advantage of their new, somewhat unexpected ally. As an example one may cite Bishop Butler, who shows how "reasonable self-love"—that is interest—is arrayed alongside morality *against* the passions:

> . . . particular passions are no more coincident with prudence, or that reasonable self-love, the end of which is our worldly interest, than they are with the principle of virtue and religion; . . . such particular passions are as much temptations to act imprudently with regard to our worldly interest, as to act viciously.[40]

For the Prince, then, the new doctrine was nearly as constraining as the old one. Moreover, it soon revealed itself as rather unhelpful: whereas the traditional standards of virtuous behavior were difficult to *attain*, interest turned out to be correspondingly difficult to *define*. It was easy enough to say in general that the interest of a king is to maintain and increase the power and wealth of his realm, but this principle hardly yielded precise "decision rules" in concrete situations.

The history of attempts to lay down such rules is tortuous and frustrating, as Meinecke has masterfully shown. Yet, although the concept of interest became fairly bogged down in its original domain (the prince or state), it prospered remarkably when it was applied to groups or individuals within the state. Here the mixture of self-seeking and rationality that had been developed as the quintessence of interest-motivated behavior in the discussions around statecraft was found to be a particularly useful *and* hopeful category.

The transition from the *interest* of the ruler to the *interests* of various groups among the ruled proceeded in somewhat different ways in England and France. In England the concept of interest in the singular that was to guide princes and statesmen and later turned into the "national interest" was apparently imported from France and Italy early in the seventeenth century.[m] Rohan's *On the Interest of Princes and States of Christendom* was particularly influential. It was rapidly translated and provoked much comment. One of Rohan's pithy phrases in his opening paragraph—*l'intérêt seul ne peut jamais manquer* (coming after *Le prince peut se tromper, son Conseil peut être corrompu, mais . . .*)—is at the origin of the maxim "Interest Will Not Lie," which gained considerable currency in seventeenth-century England.[n]

In his essay Rohan had defined interest in terms of dynastic or foreign policy. It was revolution and civil war in mid-seventeenth-century England that necessar-

[m] J. A. W. Gunn, *Politics and the Public Interest in the Seventeenth Century* (London: Routledge and Kegan Paul, 1969), p. 36 and passim. I have much profited from the wealth of information contained in this volume on the concept of "interest" and "interests" in seventeenth-century England. See also Gunn's article " 'Interest Will Not Lie': A Seventeenth-Century Political Maxim," *Journal of the History of Ideas* 29 (Oct.-Dec. 1968), pp. 551–564. An excellent analysis of related topics is in Felix Raab, *The English Face of Machiavelli: A Changing Interpretation, 1500–1700* (London: Routledge and Kegan Paul, 1964), pp. 157–158.

[n] The maxim was used as the title of an important pamphlet by Marchamont Nedham, a vicar and expertly flexible politician as well as a great admirer of, and frequent borrower from, both Machiavelli and Rohan. See the just cited works by Gunn and Raab.

ily imparted more of a domestic and group orientation to the concept. The "interest of England" was no longer discussed in relation to Spain or France, but rather in relation to the main protagonists of those domestic struggles. Similarly, after the Restoration, the discussions around religious tolerance dealt with the interest of England in relation to the interests of Presbyterians, Catholics, Quakers, and others. It was thereafter, toward the end of the century, with political stability reestablished and a measure of religious toleration ensured, that the interests of groups and individuals were increasingly discussed in terms of economic aspirations.[o] By the early eighteenth century we find Shaftesbury defining interest as the "desire of those conveniences, by which we are well provided for, and maintained" and speaking of the "possession of wealth" as "that passion which is esteemed peculiarly *interesting*."[41] Hume similarly uses the terms "passion of interest" or the "interested affection" as synonyms for the "avidity of acquiring goods and possessions" or the "love of gain."[42] This evolution of the term may have been assisted by a convergent shift in the meaning of "public interest"; "plenty" became an increasingly important ingredient of that expression.[p]

[o] Raab writes at the end of a long bibliographical footnote on "Interest": "It was at the end of this period [that is, in the last decade of the seventeenth century] that 'interest' acquired a specifically economic . . . meaning." *The English Face of Machiavelli*, p. 237. Gunn says more generally: "Interest made the journey from the council chambers to the market place very quickly." *Politics*, p. 42.

[p] Gunn, *Politics*, Chapter 5 and p. 265. This is not incompatible with Viner's well-known demonstration that power and plenty were twin foreign policy objectives of equal standing throughout the mercantilist epoch. See Jacob Viner, "Power versus Plenty as Objectives of Foreign Policy in the Seventeenth and Eighteenth

In France the political conditions of *le grand siècle* were hardly favorable to a systematic consideration of private or group interests in their relation to the public interest. Nevertheless, the career of the term *intérêt* resembled that of its English cousin. The idea of interest as it had been developed by the political literature since Machiavelli—the idea, that is, of a disciplined understanding of what it takes to advance one's power, influence, and wealth—came into common use early in the seventeenth century and was soon utilized by the great moralists and other writers of the period in their meticulous dissection of individual human nature. As the scene these writers were dealing with was typically the court of Louis XIV, the actors were "interested" in much the same categories as the sovereign himself: not only in wealth, but also and perhaps principally in power and influence. Hence interest was often used with a very inclusive meaning. Yet even then—and this is the point of convergence of the English and French histories—that meaning was being narrowed, by some process, to the pursuit of material, economic advantage. This can be inferred from the "Advice to the Reader" by which La Rochefoucauld prefaced the second edition (1666) of his *Maximes*:

> By the word interest I understand not always an interest concerned with wealth (*un intérêt de bien*), but most frequently one that is concerned with honor or glory.[43]

This warning against misunderstanding was the only point of real substance in a very short preface; clearly,

---

Centuries," *World Politics*, Vol. 1 (1948), reprinted in D. C. Coleman, ed., *Revisions in Mercantilism* (London: Methuen, 1969), pp. 61–91.

38

for the average reader of the *Maximes,* the term "interest" had started to take on the more restricted sense of economic advantage.

Around the same time Jean de Silhon, Richelieu's secretary and apologist, also noted and deplored this evolution of meaning in a treatise in which he underlines the positive role played by interest in maintaining life and society. He lists a variety of interests—"Interest of conscience, Interest of honor, Interest of health, Interest of wealth, and several other Interests"—and then attributes the unfavorable connotation attaching to such expressions as *un homme intéressé* to the fact that "the name of Interest has remained attached exclusively, I do not know how *(je ne sais comment),* to the Interest of wealth *(Intérêt du bien ou des richesses)."*[44]

How, in fact, can this drift be explained? Perhaps it was due to the old association of interest and money-lending; this meaning of interest antedates the one that is discussed here by several centuries. Possibly, too, the special affinity of rational calculation implicit in the concept of interest with the nature of economic activities accounts for these activities eventually monopolizing the contents of the concept. Returning to seventeenth-century France, one may also conjecture that, with power so concentrated and seemingly so stable at the time, economic interests constituted the only portion of an ordinary person's total aspirations in which important ups and downs could be visualized.

Actually Adam Smith stated the last point as a general proposition when discussing what he considered the overriding motive of man, namely, the "desire of bettering our condition":

An augmentation of fortune is the means by which the greater part of men propose and wish to better their condition. It is the means the most vulgar and the most obvious. . . .[45]

Perhaps no other explanation is needed for the narrowing of the meaning of the term "interests" once the beginnings of economic growth made the "augmentation of fortune" a real possibility for an increasing number of people.[q]

So much is clear now: when the interests of men came to be contrasted with their passions, this opposition could have quite different meanings depending on whether interests were understood in the wider or in the narrower sense. A maxim such as "Interest Will Not Lie" was originally an exhortation to pursue *all* of one's aspirations in an orderly and reasonable manner; it advocated the injection of an element of calculating efficiency, as well as of prudence, into human behavior whatever might be the passion by which it is basically motivated. But because of the just noted semantic drift of the term "interests," the opposition between interests and passions could also mean or convey a different thought, much more startling in view of traditional

[q] "Corruption" has had a similar semantic trajectory. In the writings of Machiavelli, who took the term from Polybius, *corruzione* stood for deterioration in the quality of government, no matter for what reason it may occur. The term was still used with this inclusive meaning in eighteenth-century England, although it became also identified with bribery at that time. Eventually the monetary meaning drove the nonmonetary one out almost completely. This is also what happened with the term "fortune," which Adam Smith uses, in the passage just cited, in the strict monetary sense in contrast to the much wider meaning of *fortuna* in Machiavelli. See J. G. A. Pocock, "Machiavelli, Harrington, and English Political Ideologies in the Eighteenth Century," *William and Mary Quarterly* 22 (Oct. 1965), pp. 568–571, and *The Machiavellian Moment* (Princeton, N.J.: Princeton University Press, 1975), p. 405.

values: namely, that *one set of passions, hitherto known variously as greed, avarice, or love of lucre, could be usefully employed to oppose and bridle such other passions as ambition, lust for power, or sexual lust.*

At this point, then, a junction is effected between the previously developed train of thought on countervailing passions and the doctrine of interest. Both doctrines originated in Machiavelli; yet the final outcome—the promotion of avarice to the position of the privileged passion given the job of taming the wild ones and of making in this fashion a crucial contribution to statecraft—would have greatly surprised and outraged him. In a well-known letter to his friend Francesco Vettori, Machiavelli left no doubt about his belief that economics and politics dwell in two separate spheres:

> Fortune has decreed that, as I do not know how to reason, either about the art of silk, or about the art of wool, either about profits or about losses, it befits me to reason about the State.[46]

What holds for Machiavelli is true also for many others who had forged important links in the chain of reasoning here described. In general the story told up to now illustrates how unintended consequences flow from human thought (and from the shape it is given through language) no less than from human actions. In the numerous treatises on the passions that appeared in the seventeenth century, no change whatever can be found in the assessment of avarice as the "foulest of them all" or in its position as the deadliest Deadly Sin that it had come to occupy toward the end of the Middle Ages.[47] But once money-making wore the label of "interests" and reentered in this disguise the competition with the other passions, it was suddenly acclaimed and even given the task of holding back those passions that had long been thought to be much less reprehensible. To account for this reversal it does not seem enough to point out that a new, comparatively neutral, and colorless term permitted lifting or attenuating the stigma attached to the old labels. A stronger explanation is provided by our demonstration that the term "interests" actually carried—and therefore bestowed on money-making—a *positive* and *curative* connotation deriving from its recent close association with the idea of a more enlightened way of conducting human affairs, private as well as public.

Interest as a New Paradigm

THE idea of an opposition between interests and passions made its first appearance, to my knowledge, with the previously noted work of Rohan, which is wholly concerned with rulers and statesmen. In subsequent decades the dichotomy was discussed by a number of English and French writers who applied it to human conduct in general.

The occasion for the discussion was a phenomenon that is familiar in intellectual history: once the idea of interest had appeared, it became a real fad as well as a paradigm (à la Kuhn) and most of human action was suddenly explained by self-interest, sometimes to the point of tautology. La Rochefoucauld dissolved the passions *and* almost all virtues into self-interest, and in England Hobbes carried out a similar reductionist enterprise. In line with these developments the original maxim "Interest Will Not Lie," which had the normative meaning that interest should be carefully figured out and then be followed in preference to other conceivable courses of action inspired by different motives, turned by the end of the century into the positive proverb "Interest Governs the World."[48] The infatuation with interest as a key to the understanding of human action carried over into the eighteenth century when Helvétius, in spite of his exaltation of the passions, proclaimed:

> As the physical world is ruled by the laws of movement so is the moral universe ruled by laws of interest.[49]

As happens frequently with concepts that are suddenly thrust to the center of the stage—class, elite, economic development, to name some more recent examples— interest appeared so self-evident a notion that nobody bothered to define it precisely. Nor did anyone explain the place it occupied in relation to the two categories that had dominated the analysis of human motivation since Plato, namely, the passions on the one hand, and reason on the other. But it is precisely against the background of this traditional dichotomy that the emergence of a third category in the late sixteenth and early seventeenth century can be understood. Once passion was deemed destructive and reason ineffectual, the view that human action could be exhaustively described by attribution to either one or the other meant an exceedingly somber outlook for humanity. A message of hope was therefore conveyed by the wedging of interest in between the two traditional categories of human motivation. Interest was seen to partake in effect of the better nature of each, as the passion of self-love upgraded and contained by reason, and as reason given direction and force by that passion. The resulting hybrid form of human action was considered exempt from both the destructiveness of passion and the ineffectuality of reason. No wonder that the doctrine of interest was received at the time as a veritable message of salvation! The specific reasons for its considerable appeal will be examined in detail in the next section.[r]

Not everybody was convinced of course that all problems had been solved. There were those, in the first place, who resisted the blandishments of the new doctrine and rejected it outright. As an ardent admirer of St. Augustine, Bossuet saw little to choose between passion and interest. For him both "interest and passion corrupt man," and he warns against the temptations of the royal court as both "the empire of interest" and the "theater of the passions."[50]

But so negative a stance was the exception. In general the critics of the new doctrine merely doubted that interest, in the sense of reasonable, deliberate "self-love," could be a match for the passions. Such was Spinoza's view:

> All men certainly seek their advantage, but seldom as sound reason dictates; in most cases appetite is their only guide, and in their desires and judgments of what is beneficial they are carried away by their passions, which take no account of the future or of anything else.[51]

Elsewhere one finds the preeminence of interest contested, not so much because of the overpowering inter-

---

[r] Louis Hartz is therefore taking an unhistorical view when he speaks of the "liberal bleakness about man which sees him working autonomously on the basis of his own self-interest" and contrasts this pessimistic view of human nature with the "feudal bleakness about man which sees him fit only for external domination." *The Liberal Tradition in America* (New York: Harcourt, Brace and World, 1955), p. 80. Originally the idea that man is ruled by interest was not sensed as bleak at all.

ference of the passions, as simply because of the inability of men to perceive their interests. But the inference was again that a state in which interests would be clearly perceived and followed would be most enviable, as in this ironical remark of the Marquis of Halifax:

> If men must be supposed always to follow their true interest, it must be meant of a new manufactory of mankind by God Almighty; there must be some new clay, the old stuff never yet made any such infallible creature.[52]

In France Cardinal de Retz paid his respects to the new doctrine, but cautioned with fine psychological acumen against counting the passions out:

> The most correct maxim for accurately appraising the intentions of men is to examine their interests which are the most common motive for their actions. But a truly subtle politician does not wholly reject the conjectures which one can derive from man's passions, for passions enter sometimes rather openly into, and almost always manage to affect unconsciously, the motives that propel the most important affairs of state.[s]

[s] Cardinal de Retz, *Mémoires* (Paris: Pléiade, NRF, 1956), pp. 1008–1009. Elsewhere Retz writes similarly: "In the times . . . in which we live one must join the inclinations of men with their interests and draw on this mixture in order to make a judgment on their probable behavior." *Ibid.*, p. 984. A strikingly similar opinion is expressed over a century later by Alexander Hamilton, another practicing (and reflective) politician: "Though nations, in the main, are governed by what they suppose their interest, he must be imperfectly versed in human nature who . . . does not know that [kind or unkind] dispositions may insensibly mould or bias the views of self-interest." Cited in Gerald Stourzh, *Alexander Hamilton and the Idea of Republican Government* (Stanford, Calif.: Stanford University Press, 1970), p. 92.

Like Spinoza and Halifax, Retz still seems to feel here that the intrusion of the passions makes the world into a less orderly place than it would be if it were ruled by interest alone. A few decades later La Bruyère roughly agrees with Retz on the weight to be assigned to the interests and the passions as determinants of human behavior and at the same time explicitly recognizes the existence of the new *ménage à trois*:

> Nothing is easier for passion than to defeat reason: Its great triumph is to gain the upper hand over interest.[53]

It is perhaps significant that La Bruyère strikes here a posture of clinical detachment; in contrast to the previously quoted opinions, he expresses no dismay whatsoever at the occasional victory of the passions over the interests.

In the eighteenth century the view that interest is paramount was subjected to much stronger criticism. Here are two typical statements, the first by Shaftesbury, and the second by Bishop Butler:

> You have heard it . . . as a common saying that *Interest governs the World*. But, I believe, whoever looks narrowly into the affairs of it, will find that *passion, humour, caprice, zeal, faction*, and a thousand other springs, which are counter to *self-interest*, have as considerable a part in the movements of this machine.[54]

> We daily see [reasonable self-love] overmatched, not only by the more boisterous passions, but by curiosity, shame, love of imitation, by anything, even indolence; especially if the interest, the temporal interest which is the end of such self-love, be at a

distance. So greatly are profligate men mistaken when they affirm they are wholly governed by interestedness and self-love.[55]

The new emphasis of these two passages must be interpreted in the light of a considerable change that took place in the attitude toward the passions from the seventeenth to the eighteenth century. They were first viewed as wholly vicious and destructive, as in the following phrase from a French catechism: "The Kingdom of France is not a tyranny, where the Sovereign's conduct would be guided solely by his passion."[56] But gradually, toward the end of the seventeenth and more fully in the course of the eighteenth century, the passions were rehabilitated as the essence of life and as a potentially creative force. In the earlier period, when the proposition that man's conduct is wholly shaped by his interests was criticized on the ground that passion still had to be taken into account, the criticism assumed that the world is a *worse* place than that proposition implied. But with the rehabilitation of the passions in the eighteenth century, the identical criticism could then mean that a world in which the passions are active and prevail on occasion is a *better* place than one in which interest alone would call the tune. The juxtaposition of passion by Shaftesbury and Butler with such harmless and even useful emotions as humor and curiosity suggests this interpretation. It is rooted in the rejection, by the Enlightenment, of the tragic and pessimistic view of man and society that was so characteristic of the seventeenth century. The new view, which sees the passions as *improving* a world governed by interest alone, is fully articulated by Hume:

. . . reasons of state, which are supposed solely to influence the councils of monarchs are not always the motives which there predominate; . . . the milder views of gratitude, honour, friendship, generosity, are frequently able, among princes as well as private persons, to counterbalance these selfish considerations.[57]

Naturally, once the meaning of interests was narrowed to material advantage, the idea that "Interest Governs the World" was bound to lose much of its earlier appeal. In fact, the phrase turns into a lament, or into a denunciation of cynicism, when a character in Schiller's play *Wallenstein's Tod* exclaims:

Denn nur vom Nutzen wird die Welt regiert.[t]

This is clearly a translation of the seventeenth-century proverb, which Schiller was probably keen on bringing into a play that dealt with events of that period. The only trouble was that the derogatory meaning he imparted to the saying—in line with eighteenth-century ideological currents—was totally different from the one it had at the time of Wallenstein!

Assets of an Interest-Governed World: Predictability and Constancy

THE belief that interest could be considered a dominant motive of human behavior caused considerable intellectual excitement: at last a realistic basis for a viable social order had been discovered. But a world

[t] Act I, Scene 6, Line 37. "For the world is ruled by nothing but interest." The change of meaning from the proverb is here strongly assisted by the insertion of the word "nur"—"only" or "nothing but."

governed by interest offered not only an escape from excessively demanding models of states that "have never been seen nor have been known to exist"; it was perceived to have a number of specific assets of its own.

The most general of these assets was *predictability*. Machiavelli had shown that some powerful propositions about politics can be extracted from the assumption of a uniform human nature.[58] But his diagnosis was far too pessimistic to be widely adopted—witness the admittedly extreme formulation in Chapter 17 of *The Prince* according to which men are "ungrateful, voluble, false, hypocritical, cowardly, greedy." The idea of men being invariably guided by their interests could command much wider acceptance, and whatever slight distaste the idea left behind was then dispelled by the comforting thought that in this manner the world became a more predictable place. The pamphlet "Interest Will Not Lie" stressed this point:

> If you can apprehend wherein a man's interest to any particular game on foot doth consist you may surely know, if the man be prudent, whereabout to have him, that is, how to judge of his design.[59]

Similar ideas can be found in the post-Restoration literature advocating religious toleration. One tract says:

> . . . to surmise the acting of multitudes, contrary to their own interests—is to take all assurance out of humane affairs.[60]

Later Sir James Steuart was to use the same reasoning to argue that individual behavior governed by self-interest is preferable not only to the rule of the passions but even to virtuous behavior and, particularly, to concern for the public interest among the "governed":

49

Were miracles wrought every day, the laws of nature would no longer be laws: and were everyone to act for the public, and neglect himself, the statesman would be bewildered. . . .

. . . were a people to become quite disinterested: there would be no possibility of governing them. Everyone might consider the interest of his country in a different light, and many might join in the ruin of it, by endeavoring to promote its advantages.[61]

On the one hand, therefore, if a man pursues his interest, he himself will do well since, by definition, "interest will not lie to him or deceive him"[62]—that was the very meaning of the proverb. On the other hand, there is an advantage for others in his pursuing his interest, for his course of action becomes thereby transparent and predictable almost as though he were a wholly virtuous person. In this fashion the possibility of a mutual gain emerged from the expected working of interest *in politics*, quite some time before it became a matter of doctrine in economics.

There were of course a number of serious difficulties with this notion. For one, the modern objection that unpredictability is power was already voiced at the time. While generally adhering to the doctrine of interest, Samuel Butler held that foolish and incapable persons in government

have one advantage, above those that are wiser, and that of no mean importance; for no man can guess, nor imagine, beforehand, what course they will probably take in any business that occurs, when 'tis not uneasy to foresee, by their interests, what wiser men are like in reason to design.[63]

A more weighty objection to the possibility of a mutual gain arising from a situation in which all parties steadfastly pursue their interests derived from the fact that in international politics the interests of the principal parties are often exactly opposite to one another. That the interests of one power are the mirror image of the interests of its chief rival was shown, for example, for France and Spain in Rohan's essay to the point of tedium. Even in these circumstances, however, something was thought to be gained for both parties by the adherence to certain rules of the game and by the elimination of "passionate" behavior, which the rational pursuit of interest implied.

The probability of an all-round gain became somewhat higher when the doctrine was applied to domestic politics. Like the term "interest" itself, the notion of a *balance* of interests was transferred in England from its original context involved with statecraft—where it yielded the concept of a "balance of power"—to the conflict-ridden domestic scene. After the Restoration and during the debate on religious toleration, there was much discussion about the advantages that might accrue to the public interest from the presence of a variety of interests and from a certain tension between them.[64]

But the benefits to be derived from the predictability of human conduct based on interest loomed largest when the concept was used in connection with the economic activities of individuals. If only because of the large number of actors, the opposition of interests involved in trade could not be nearly so total, conspicuous, or threatening as it could for two neighboring states or for a few rival political or confessional groups within states. The by-product of individuals acting predictably in accordance with their economic interests was therefore not an uneasy *balance*, but a strong *web* of inter-dependent relationships. Thus it was expected that expansion of domestic trade would create more cohesive communities while foreign trade would help avoid wars between them.

A brief remark on the historiography of economic doctrines may be inserted here. Writings on mercantilist doctrine have accredited the idea that economic thinking prior to Hume and Adam Smith considered trade as strictly a zero-sum game, with the gain accruing to the country with an excess of exports over imports while an equivalent loss is suffered by the country in the opposite position. But anyone looking at the whole range of considerations on commerce and trade expressed in seventeenth- and eighteenth-century writings, rather than only at the discussion about the trade balance, will conclude that *all-round* beneficial effects were widely expected to flow from the expansion of commerce. Many of these effects were political, social, and even moral rather than purely economic, and a number of them will be reviewed in the following sections of this essay.

Predictability in its most elementary form is constancy, and it is this quality that was perhaps the most important ground for welcoming a world governed by interest. The erratic and fluctuating character of most passionate behavior had often been stressed and was considered one of its most objectionable and dangerous features. The passions were "divers" (Hobbes), capricious, easily exhausted and suddenly renewed again. According to Spinoza,

> Men may differ in nature from one another insofar as they are agitated by . . . passions, and insofar as one and the same man is agitated by passions is he changeable and inconstant.[65]

Inconstancy actually came to the fore as a central difficulty in creating a viable social order after Machiavelli's and Hobbes's extreme pessimism about human nature (and about the resulting "state of nature") gave way to more moderate views in the second half of the seventeenth century. One of the major social contract doctrines of the seventeenth century, that of Pufendorf, still made some reference, in the manner of Hobbes, to the "insatiable desire and ambition" of man, but based the need for a covenant primarily on man's inconstancy and untrustworthiness, on the fact "that the typical relationship of one man to another was that of 'an inconstant friend.' "[66]

This doctrine was essentially embraced by Locke, who had explicitly acknowledged Pufendorf's influence on his political thought.[67] Locke constructed a state of nature that is, if not "idyllic" as some critics have put it, at least remarkably nonprimitive, alive as it is with private property, inheritance, commerce, and even money. But precisely because of this oddly "advanced" character of Locke's state of nature there is need to secure it firmly through a compact that will ensure the permanence of its achievements. The Lockean compact is meant to remove the "inconveniences, that [men] are exposed to [in the state of nature], by the irregular and uncertain exercise of the Power every Man has of punishing the transgression of others. . . ."[68] Elsewhere Locke says that "Freedom of Men under Government" means "not to be subject to the inconstant, uncertain, unknown, Arbitrary Will of another man."[69] Uncertainty in general and man's inconstancy in particular therefore become the arch-enemy that needs to be exorcised. Although Locke does not appeal to interest to keep inconstancy at bay, there is clearly an affinity between the

Commonwealth he is attempting to construct and the seventeenth-century image of a world ruled by interest. For in the pursuit of their interests men were expected or assumed to be steadfast, single-minded, and methodical, in total contrast to the stereotyped behavior of men who are buffeted and blinded by their passions.

This aspect of the matter also helps us understand the eventual identification of interest in its original broad sense with one particular passion, the love of money. For the perceived characteristics of this passion, which set it apart from others, were precisely constancy, doggedness, and sameness from one day to the next and from one person to another. In one of his essays Hume speaks of avarice—without bothering to disguise it as "interest"—as an "obstinate passion";[70] in another he elaborates:

> Avarice, or the desire of gain, is a universal passion which operates at all times, in all places, and upon all persons.[u]

In the *Treatise* Hume had specifically contrasted the "love of gain," which is characterized as "perpetual" and "universal," with other passions, such as envy and revenge, that "operate only by intervals, and are directed against particular persons."[v] Another comparative ap-

[u] *Essays Moral, Political, and Literary*, ed. T. H. Green and T. H. Grose (London: Longmans, 1898), Vol. I, p. 176. Compare this to Hume's description of love in another essay: "Love is a restless and impatient passion, full of caprice and variations: arising in a moment from a feature, from an air, from nothing, and suddenly extinguishing after the same manner" (p. 238).

[v] *A Treatise of Human Nature*, Book III, Part II, Section II. This comparative appraisal is made in the context of Hume's account for the existence of civil society, and the strength and universality of the desire of gain are first presented as a threat to society. Hume then shows how this threat is averted "upon the

praisal of avarice is given by Samuel Johnson in *Rasselas, Prince of Abyssinia,* where a lady-in-waiting at the court tells of her captivity:

> My condition had lost much of its terror since I found that the Arab ranged the country merely to get riches. Avarice is a uniform and tractable vice; other intellectual distempers are different in different constitutions of mind; that which soothes the pride of one will offend the pride of another; but to the favor of the covetous there is a ready way: bring money and nothing is denied.[71]

The remarkable constancy and persistence of the passion of accumulation is also noted by Montesquieu:

> One commerce leads to another: the small to the medium; the medium to the large; and the person who was so anxious to make a little money places himself in a situation in which he is no less anxious to make a lot.[72]

Here Montesquieu seems to marvel at money's being an exception to what became known in modern economics as the law of decreasing marginal utility. About one hundred fifty years later the German sociologist Georg Simmel made some illuminating remarks on this very subject. Normally, he said, the fulfilment of human desire means an intimate acquaintance with all the diverse facets of the desired object or experience, and this acquaintance is responsible for the well-known dissonance between desire and fulfilment, which takes most frequently the form of disappointment; but the desire for any given amount of money, once satisfied, is

---

least reflection; since 'tis evident that the passion is much better satisfied by its restraint. . . ." See above, p. 25.

uniquely immune to this disappointment *provided that money is not spent on things, but that its accumulation becomes an end in itself*: for then "as a thing absolutely devoid of quality, [money] cannot harbor either surprise or disappointment as does any object, however miserable."[73] Simmel's psychological explanation might have appealed to Hume, Montesquieu, and Dr. Johnson, who were obviously intrigued by the constancy of the love of money, so peculiar a quality in a passion.

The *insatiability* of *auri sacra fames* had often been considered the most dangerous and reprehensible aspect of that passion. By a strange twist, because of the preoccupation of post-Hobbesian thinking with man's inconstancy, this very insatiability now became a virtue because it implied constancy. Nevertheless, for this radical change in valuation to carry conviction, and to effectuate a temporary suspension of deeply rooted patterns of thought and judgment, it was necessary to endow the "obstinate" desire for gain with an additional quality: harmlessness.

Money-Making and Commerce as Innocent and *Doux*

THE insight about the characteristic persistence of the "interested affection" (Hume) is rather apt to strike the modern reader as alarming, because he will immediately think of the likelihood that a drive so powerfully endowed would sweep everything else out of its path. This reaction found its most vigorous and famous articulation a century later, in the *Communist Manifesto*. To be sure, some notes of alarm were sounded

already in early eighteenth-century England where the
Bank crisis of 1710, the South Sea Bubble of 1720, and
the widespread political corruption of the age of Walpole gave rise to concerns that the old order was being
undermined by money. Bolingbroke, Walpole's Tory
adversary, launched a few attacks on the stockjobbers
and the powerful *nouveaux riches* of his day and even
came to denounce, in his newspaper, *The Craftsman,*
the role that money was occupying as "a more lasting tie
than honour, friendship, relation, consanguinity, or
unity of affections."ᵂ But these feelings were to assume
some ideological importance only well into the second
half of the century among the Scottish writers, particularly Adam Ferguson, and in France with Mably and
Morelly. During much of the century, in both England
and France, the dominant appraisal of the "love of gain"
was positive, if somewhat disdainful, as in the above
quoted passage from *Rasselas* (". . . the Arab ranged
the country *merely* to get riches").

Dr. Johnson is also responsible for a related, famous,
and, in our context, particularly revealing remark:

ᵂ Cited in Isaac Kramnick, *Bolingbroke and his Circle: The
Politics of Nostalgia in the Age of Walpole* (Cambridge, Mass.:
Harvard University Press, 1968), p. 73; see Chapter III in general
for a presentation of Bolingbroke as an early "populist" politician. Kramnick may have overdrawn this picture—at the end of
Chapter III he has to rely on Hume for the most telling indictment of some of the financial innovations of the period. For a
different view of Bolingbroke's opposition, see Quentin Skinner,
"The Principles and Practice of Opposition: The Case of Bolingbroke versus Walpole," in Neil McKendrick, ed., *Historical Per-
spectives: Studies in English Thought and Society in Honour of
J. H. Plumb* (London: Europa, 1974), pp. 93–218; and J. G. A.
Pocock, "Machiavelli," pp. 577–578. Pocock argues that Bolingbroke was exercised less over the rise of the market than over the
power that the Court and the Prime Minister could wield as a
result of the enlarged financial resources at their disposal.

> There are few ways in which a man can be more innocently employed than in getting money.[74]

This epigram spells out another count on which interest-motivated behavior and money-making were considered to be superior to ordinary passion-oriented behavior. The passions were wild and dangerous, whereas looking after one's material interests was innocent or, as one would say today, innocuous. This is a little known yet particularly revealing component of the complex of ideas under discussion.

The evaluation of commercial and money-making pursuits as harmless and innocuous can be understood as an indirect consequence of the long-dominant aristocratic ideal. As noted earlier, when the faith in this ideal had been severely shaken and the "hero" had been "demolished," the long-maligned trader did not correspondingly rise in prestige: the idea that he was a mean, grubby, and uninspiring fellow lingered for a long time.

There even was doubt that commerce was an efficient instrument in relation to its own money-making objectives—a doubt expressed as late as the mid-eighteenth century by Vauvenargues in the surprising maxim: "Interest makes few fortunes."[75] That "a man of quality, by fighting, acquires wealth more honorably *and quickly* than a meaner man by work" has been called a basic belief of the Spaniards as they emerged from the Reconquest,[76] but the idea was widely shared. The very contempt in which economic activities were held led to the conviction, in spite of much evidence to the contrary, that they could not possibly have much potential in any area of human endeavor and were incapable of causing either good *or evil* on a grand scale. In an age in which men were searching for ways of limiting the damage and horrors they are wont to inflict on each other, commercial and economic activities were therefore looked upon more kindly not because of any rise in the esteem in which they were held; on the contrary, any preference for them expressed a desire for a vacation from (disastrous) greatness, and thus reflected continuing contempt. In a sense, the triumph of capitalism, like that of many modern tyrants, owes much to the widespread refusal to take it seriously or to believe it capable of great design or achievement, a refusal so evident in Dr. Johnson's remark.

The Johnsonian epigram about the innocuousness of "money getting" had its counterpart in France. In fact, the identical term "innocent" can be found as a characterization of commercial activities in the preamble of the 1669 edict that declared seaborne commerce to be compatible with nobility:

> Whereas Commerce is the fertile source which brings abundance to the states and spreads it among its subjects . . .; and whereas no way of acquiring wealth is more innocent and more legitimate. . . .[77]

Subsequently another, at first sight even odder term caught on. There was much talk, from the late seventeenth century on, about the *douceur* of commerce: a word notoriously difficult to translate into other languages (as, for example, in *la douce France*), it conveys sweetness, softness, calm, and gentleness and is the antonym of violence. The first mention of this qualification of commerce I have been able to find occurs in Jacques Savary's *Le parfait négociant*, the seventeenth-century textbook for businessmen:

> [Divine Providence] has not willed for everything that is needed for life to be found in the same spot. It has dispersed its gifts so that men would trade

59

together and so that the mutual need which they
have to help one another would establish ties of
friendship among them. *This continuous exchange
of all the comforts of life constitutes commerce and
this commerce makes for all the gentleness* (douceur) *of life. . . .*[78]

This passage first expounds the idea of a "favorable interest of providence in international trade" that Jacob
Viner has traced to the fourth century A.D.[79] But the
last sentence on *douceur,* underlined by Savary, belongs
very much to the era in which he wrote.

The most influential exponent of the doctrine of the
doux commerce was Montesquieu. In the part of *Esprit
des lois* that deals with economic matters he states in
the opening chapter:

. . . it is almost a general rule that wherever the
ways of man are gentle (*mœurs douces*) there is
commerce; and wherever there is commerce, there
the ways of men are gentle.[80]

And later in the same chapter he repeats:

Commerce . . . polishes and softens (*adoucit*) bar-
barian ways as we can see every day.

It is not very clear in Montesquieu whether the *douceur*-inducing effect of commerce is supposed to be
brought about by the changes commerce works among
the people engaging in trading activities or, more amply,
among all those who use and consume the commodities
made available through commerce. In any event, the
term in its widest meaning had a successful career outside France. Twenty-one years after the publication of
Montesquieu's work the just cited phrase is found al-

most verbatim in the work of the Scottish historian William Robertson, who writes in his *View of the Progress of Society in Europe* (1769):

> Commerce tends to wear off those prejudices which maintain distinctions and animosity between nations. It *softens and polishes* the manners of men.[x]

The expression "the polished nations," in contradistinction to the "rude and barbarous" ones, came to be commonly used in England and Scotland toward the second half of the eighteenth century. It designated the countries of Western Europe whose increasing wealth was clearly perceived to have much to do with the expansion of commerce. The term "polished" may well have been selected because of its affinity with *adouci*: in this manner the *douceur* of commerce could have been indirectly responsible for the first attempt at expressing a dichotomy that reappeared later under such labels as "advanced-backward," "developed-underdeveloped," and so on.

The origin of the epithet *doux* is probably to be found in the "noncommercial" meaning of *commerce*: besides trade the word long denoted animated and repeated conversation and other forms of polite social intercourse and dealings among persons (frequently between two persons of the opposite sex).[y] It was in this

[x] This work, which is the preface to Robertson's *History of the Reign of the Emperor Charles V*, has recently been edited and supplied with an introduction by Felix Gilbert (University of Chicago Press, 1972). The cited passage (emphasis mine) is on p. 67. In the "Proofs and Illustrations" appended to his essay Robertson refers to Montesquieu's introduction to the part of *Esprit des lois* that deals with commerce (see p. 165), though not to the precise phrase he adopts from that work.

[y] This is true for English as well as for French. See the *Oxford English Dictionary*.

connection that the term *doux* was often used in conjunction with *commerce*. For example, the internal rules of a Parisian *collège* issued in 1769 contain the sentence:

> As they are to live in society upon leaving the *Collège*, the pupils will be trained at an early stage in the practice of a gentle, easy and honest intercourse (*un commerce doux, aisé et honnête*).[81]

The term thus carried into its "commercial" career an overload of meaning that denoted politeness, polished manners, and socially useful behavior in general. Even so, the persistent use of the term *le doux commerce* strikes us as a strange aberration for an age when the slave trade was at its peak and when trade in general was still a hazardous, adventurous, and often violent business.[z] A century later the term was duly ridiculed by Marx who, in accounting for the primitive accumulation of capital, recounts some of the more violent episodes in the history of European commercial expansion and then exclaims sarcastically: "Das ist der *doux commerce!*"[aa]

---

[z] The trade-and-exchange-conscious Savary was able to come to terms with the institution of slavery by pointing out that the "cultivation of tobacco, sugar and indigo . . . does not fail to be advantageous" to the slaves because of "the knowledge of the true God and of Christian religion which is supplied to them as a kind of compensation for the loss of liberty." Cited in E. Levasseur, *Histoire du commerce de la France* (Paris: A. Rousseau, 1911), Vol. I, p. 302.

[aa] *Das Kapital*, Vol. I, Chapter 24, Section 6. The term became apparently a private joke between Marx and Engels. When the latter finally gave up, in 1869, his connection with the family textile firm in order to devote himself wholly to the socialist movement, he wrote Marx: "Hurrah! Today marks the end of the *doux commerce*, and I am a free man." Letter of July 1, 1869, in Karl Marx-Friedrich Engels, *Werke* (Berlin: Dietz, 1965), Vol. 32, p. 329.

The image of the trader as a *doux*, peaceful, inoffensive fellow may have drawn some strength from comparing him with the looting armies and murderous pirates of the time. But in France even more than in England it may also have had much to do with the lenses with which people looked at different social groups: anyone who did not belong to the nobility could not, *by definition*, share in heroic virtues or violent passions. After all, such a person had only interests and not glory to pursue, and everybody *knew* that this pursuit was bound to be *doux* in comparison to the passionate pastimes and savage exploits of the aristocracy.

Money-Making as a Calm Passion

I N THE course of the eighteenth century the positive attitude toward economic activities was bolstered by new ideological currents. Grounded though it was in the somber seventeenth-century views on human nature, it survived remarkably well the sharp attack on those views that was mounted in the succeeding age.

The earlier views on the interests and passions were subjected to several critiques. For one, as has already been shown, the proposition that man is wholly ruled by interest or self-love came to be strongly disputed. At the same time, a number of novel distinctions were made among the passions for the purpose of presenting some of them as less harmful than others, if not as outright beneficial. In this way the opposition between benign and malignant passions (with some types of acquisitive propensities classified among the former) became the eighteenth-century equivalent, especially in England, of the seventeenth-century opposition between interests and passions; but the two dichotomies over-lapped and coexisted for a prolonged period.

The new line of thought was developed, primarily in critical reaction to Hobbes's thought, by the so-called sentimental school of English and Scottish moral phil-osophers, from Shaftesbury to Hutcheson and Hume.[bb] Shaftesbury's main contribution was the rehabilitation or rediscovery of what he calls the "natural affections," such as benevolence and generosity. Distinguishing be-tween their impact on the private and on the public good, it is not difficult for him to show that these fine sen-timents serve both. Shaftesbury then addresses himself to the less admirable affections or passions and divides them into the "self-affections" or "self-passions," which are aimed at, and may lead to, the private but not neces-sarily the public good, and the "unnatural affections" (inhumanity, envy, etc.), which achieve neither public nor private good. Within each category he further dis-tinguishes between moderate and immoderate affections. It is interesting to watch what happens when he tries to fit economic activities into this conceptual scheme. He treats them under the rubric of "self-passions," but then proceeds to argue them out of it.

> If the regard toward [acquisition of wealth] be mod-erate, and in a reasonable degree; if it occasions no passionate pursuit—there is nothing in this case which is not compatible with virtue, and even suit-able and beneficial to society. But if it grows at length into a real *passion*; the injury and mischief it does the public, is not greater than that which it

[bb] Although Adam Smith was an important member of the school, his *Theory of Moral Sentiments* did not deal with the particular distinctions that Shaftesbury and Hutcheson in particu-lar treat at considerable length. He similarly ignored the distinc-tion between the passions and the interests; see below, pp. 110–112.

creates to the person himself. Such a one is in reality a self-oppressor, and lies heavier on himself than he can ever do on mankind.[82]

Obviously, then, money-making does not fit into the intermediate category of "self-passion": when pursued in moderation, it is promoted all the way to a "natural affection," which achieves both private and public good, while it is demoted to an "unnatural affection," which achieves neither, when it is indulged to excess.

Francis Hutcheson simplifies Shaftesbury's scheme and distinguishes between benevolent and selfish passions, on the one hand, and calm and violent "motions of the will," on the other. Among the few examples he gives to illustrate the latter contrast, he too cites economic activities:

> ... the calm desire of wealth will force one, tho' with reluctance, into splendid expences when necessary to gain a good bargain or a gainful employment; while the passion of avarice is repining at these expences.[83]

The criterion by which Hutcheson here divides the "calm desire of wealth" (note that "calm" is the English equivalent of *doux*) from avarice is not intensity of desire, but willingness to pay high costs to achieve even higher benefits. A calm desire is thus defined as one that acts with calculation and rationality, and is therefore exactly equivalent to what in the seventeenth century was understood by interest.

There was one problem with the new terminology: while a victory of the interests over the passions could be readily visualized, language makes it rather more difficult to see how the calm passions could come out on top in a contest with the violent ones. Hume, who had also adopted the distinction between calm and violent passions, faced the matter squarely and resolved it in one sharp sentence:

> We must . . . distinguish betwixt a calm and a weak
> passion; betwixt a violent and a strong one.[84]

In this way everything was well: an activity such as the rationally conducted acquisition of wealth could be categorized and implicitly endorsed as a calm passion that would at the same time be strong and able to triumph over a variety of turbulent (yet weak) passions. It is precisely this dual character of the acquisitive drive that Adam Smith stresses in his well-known definition of the desire of bettering our condition as "a desire which, *though generally calm and dispassionate,* comes with us from the womb, and never leaves us till we go into the grave."[85] And a specific example of this calm but strong passion gaining the upper hand over a violent one is given by Hume in his essay "Of Interest":

> It is an infallible consequence of all industrious
> professions, to . . . make the love of gain prevail
> over the love of pleasure.[86]

Even more extravagant claims on behalf of the "love of gain" will be examined shortly. But, at this point of our story, Hume's statement can stand as the culmination of the movement of ideas that has been traced: capitalism is here hailed by a leading philosopher of the age because it would activate some benign human proclivities at the expense of some malignant ones—because of the expectation that, in this way, it would repress and perhaps atrophy the more destructive and disastrous components of human nature.

PART TWO

How Economic Expansion was Expected
to Improve the Political Order

IT APPEARS that the case for giving free rein and encouragement to private acquisitive pursuits was both the outcome of a long train of Western thought and an important ingredient of the intellectual climate of the seventeenth and eighteenth centuries. If the "interests-versus-passions thesis" is nevertheless quite unfamiliar, it is so partly owing to its having been superseded and obliterated by the epochal publication, in 1776, of *The Wealth of Nations*. For reasons to be discussed, Adam Smith abandoned the distinction between the interests and the passions in making his case for the unfettered pursuit of private gain; he chose to stress the economic benefits that this pursuit would bring rather than the political dangers and disasters that it would avert.

Another reason why the thesis is unfamiliar can be inferred from the laborious way in which it had to be put together in the preceding pages from bits and pieces of intellectual evidence. By drawing on a wide range of sources I have attempted to show that the thesis was part of what Michael Polanyi has called the "tacit dimension," that is, propositions and opinions shared by a group and so obvious to it that they are never fully or systematically articulated. It is a characteristic feature of this situation that a number of important authors—including, interestingly enough, Adam Smith himself—developed special applications or variants of the non-articulated basic theory. A particularly important variant is the subject of the following pages.

As was pointed out earlier, the origins of the thesis are to be found in the concern with statecraft. The passions that most need bridling belong to the powerful, who are in a position to do harm on a huge scale and were believed to be particularly well endowed with passions in comparison to the lower orders. As a result, the most interesting applications of the thesis show how the willfulness, the disastrous lust for glory, and, in general, the passionate excesses of the powerful are curbed by the interests—their own and those of their subjects.

The principal representatives of this way of thinking in the eighteenth century were Montesquieu in France and Sir James Steuart in Scotland. Their basic ideas were enriched by John Millar, another prominent member of that remarkable group of philosophers, moralists, and social scientists sometimes referred to as the Scottish Enlightenment. The Physiocrats and Adam Smith shared some of the premises and concerns of Montesquieu and Steuart, but their solutions were very different. Except for the Physiocrats, who will be treated as the tightly unified doctrinal group they indeed were, each of these thinkers will be examined by himself. Since I shall call attention to passages in their writings that have not received much attention or scrutiny, it will be necessary to relate these passages to the rest of their work. Only in this manner is it possible to gain a perspective on the meaning and significance of the views that will be singled out here.

Elements of a Doctrine

1. MONTESQUIEU

MONTESQUIEU saw many virtues in commerce, and the relation he asserted between the expansion of commerce and the spread of gentleness (*douceur*) has already been noted. The cultural impact of commerce is for him paralleled by its political impact: in the central political Part One of *Esprit des lois,* Montesquieu argues first along classical republican lines that a democracy can ordinarily survive only when wealth is not too abundant or too unequally distributed, but he then proceeds to make an important exception to this rule for a "democracy that is based on commerce." For, he says,

the spirit of commerce brings with it the spirit of frugality, of economy, of moderation, of work, of wisdom, of tranquility, of order, and of regularity. In this manner, as long as this spirit prevails, the riches it creates do not have any bad effect.[1]

One is almost tempted to dismiss this praise of commerce because it is so extravagant. But, later in his work, Montesquieu makes a much more detailed and more closely reasoned argument on the favorable political effects of commerce. This argument has been rather neglected, and I shall now report it in some detail. It should be noted that the argument, in contrast to the one just mentioned, is not only not restricted to the effects of commerce on a democracy but applies with particular force to the two other forms of government that Montesquieu is discussing throughout his work and that he was most intimately acquainted and concerned with: monarchy and despotism.

In Part Four of *Esprit des lois* Montesquieu discusses commerce (Books XX and XXI), money (Book XXII), and population (Book XXIII). In Book XX he gives his opinion on a wide variety of general topics, from the "spirit of commerce" to the advisability of permitting the nobility to participate in commercial activities. In Book XXI, by contrast, Montesquieu deals with a single subject, the history of navigation and of commerce, and is moreover as factual as he ever manages to be. It is then the more remarkable to see him suddenly formulate a general principle in the chapter of that book in which he discusses "How Commerce Emerged in Europe from Barbarism." Montesquieu describes here first how commerce was hampered by the prohibition of interest-taking by the church and was consequently taken up by the Jews; how the Jews suffered violence and constant extortions at the hands of nobles and kings; and how eventually they reacted by inventing the bill of exchange (*lettre de change*). The final portion of the chapter draws striking conclusions:

> . . . and through this means commerce could elude violence, and maintain itself everywhere; for the richest trader had only invisible wealth which could be sent everywhere without leaving any trace. . . . In this manner we owe . . . to the avarice of rulers the establishment of a contrivance which somehow lifts commerce right out of their grip.
>
> Since that time, the rulers have been compelled to govern with greater wisdom than they themselves might have intended; for, owing to these events, the great and sudden arbitrary actions of the sovereign (*les grands coups d'autorité*) have been proven to be ineffective and . . . only good government brings prosperity [to the prince].
>
> We have begun to recover from Machiavellianism, and will continue doing so day after day. Greater moderation is needed in state councils. What used to be called coup d'état would today be nothing but imprudence, quite apart from the horror such actions inspire.

And the chapter ends with the sentence that is a crown witness for the thesis of this essay and has been chosen as its epigraph:

And it is fortunate for men to be in a situation in which, though their passions may prompt them to be wicked (méchants), *they have nevertheless an interest in not being so.*[2]

Here is a truly magnificent generalization built on the expectation that the interests—that is, commerce and its corollaries, such as the bill of exchange—would inhibit the passions and the passion-induced "wicked" actions of the powerful. A number of related passages in Montesquieu's work make it clear that the ideas he proposed in Book XXI were an important component of his thought on the relation between economics and politics.[a] He makes very much the same point in the following book (XXII) when discussing the debasement of coinage by the sovereign. The Roman emperors engaged in this practice with great relish and profit, but in more modern times debasement of coinage is counterproductive because of the extensive foreign exchange and arbitrage operations that would follow immediately:

[a] The opposition between the interests and the passions also appears elsewhere in Montesquieu's work: "Living in a state of permanent excitement, this nation could be more readily conducted by its passion than by reason—the latter never produced strong effects on men's minds; and it would be easy for those who govern that nation to have it undertake enterprises that go against its real interests." *Esprit des lois*, XIX, 27. This paragraph is from the famous chapter in which England is sympathetically portrayed at considerable length without ever being mentioned by name. As in La Bruyère (see above, p. 46), reason is here assigned the role of a comparatively impotent member in a *ménage à trois* consisting of passion, reason, and interest.

. . . these violent operations could not take place in our time; a prince would fool himself, and would not fool anybody. Foreign exchange operations (*le change*) have taught bankers to compare coins from all over the world and to assess them at their correct value. . . . These operations have done away with the great and sudden arbitrary actions of the sovereign (*les grands coups d'autorité*) or at least with their success.[3]

The two situations appear even more similar because of the almost identical terms for the two techniques that result in constraints on the politicians: the *lettre de change* in the first case, and simply *le change* in the other. In his notes Montesquieu underlines the importance of the bill of exchange—"It is astonishing that the bill of exchange has been discovered only so late, for there is nothing so useful in the world"[b]—and in *Esprit des lois* he makes much of the subdivision of wealth into land (*fonds de terre)* and movable property (*effets mobiliers*) of which the bill of exchange is part.[4]

Before Montesquieu, Spinoza had drawn the same

[b] *Mes pensées*, No. 753 in *Oeuvres complètes* (Paris: Gallimard, Pléiade edn., 1949), Vol. I, p. 1206. At the time this praise of the bill of exchange, coming after a long period of suspicion because of alleged invention by the Jews and its possible connection with usury, was by no means unusual. Half a century later, during the discussion of the Napoleonic Code of Commerce, the proponent of the section on the bill of exchange exclaimed: "The bill of exchange has been invented. In the history of commerce this is an event almost comparable to the discovery of the compass and of America. . . . [I]t has set free movable capital, has facilitated its movements, and has created an immense volume of credit. From that moment on, there have been no limits to the expansion of commerce other than those of the globe itself." Quoted in Henri Lévy-Bruhl, *Histoire de la lettre de change en France aux 17e et 18e siècles* (Paris: Sirey, 1933), p. 24.

distinction, also for political purposes, and had shown the same preference for movable over fixed capital. In the *Tractatus politicus* he went so far as to advocate state property for all real estate, including houses "if possible."[5] The purpose of the prohibition of private property was to avoid unresolvable disputes and unextinguishable envy: by owning real estate that exists in limited quantities, members of the same community are necessarily involved in a situation where one man's gain is another's loss. Therefore, it "is of great importance in promoting peace and concord . . . that no citizen is to have any real estate." Commerce and movable wealth, on the other hand, are viewed in a wholly benign light; for they give rise to "interests which are either interdependent or require the same means for their furtherance."[6] For Spinoza, the amount of money that can be owned by individuals was limited only by their efforts and these efforts in turn resulted in a network of mutual obligations, which would reinforce the ties binding society together.[7] As will be shown, the increasing importance of movable wealth in relation to land and real estate was to be used as a basis for similarly optimistic political conjectures not only by Spinoza and Montesquieu but by Sir James Steuart and Adam Smith.

Brief mention must be made here of seemingly very different attitudes toward the growth of the public debt and the consequent increase in the outstanding amount of government obligations or "public stocks." The expansion of this variety of movable wealth was considered harmful rather than beneficial by a group of English and French writers, including Hume and Montesquieu.[c]

[c] See Montesquieu, *Esprit des lois*, XXII, 17 and 18; and mainly the essay "Of Public Credit" in David Hume, *Writings on Economics*, ed. E. Rotwein (Madison, Wis.: University of Wisconsin

Although elements of a "real bills" doctrine can be found in their arguments, they criticized public debt expansion primarily on political grounds. It turns out in fact that their criticism stemmed from the same basic concern over the excesses of state power that had led them to a *positive* assessment of the increase in other types of movable wealth, such as bills of exchange. The latter types were welcomed by Montesquieu and others because they were expected to constrain the government's willingness and ability to engage in *grands coups d'autorité*. But this ability, and governmental power in general, could only be enhanced if the treasury became able to finance its operations by going into debt on a large scale. It was therefore perfectly consistent for these writers to hail increased circulation for bills of exchange while deploring it for "public stocks."

In showing how the bill of exchange and foreign exchange arbitrage make it less attractive for the powerful to act with their traditional recklessness and violence, Montesquieu does nothing but follow up on the program he had sketched out for himself in the brief essay "On Politics" written twenty-three years before the publication of *Esprit des lois*:

> It is useless to attack politics directly by showing how much its practices are in conflict with morality

Press, 1970), pp. 90–107. It is here that Hume paints a terrifying picture of the political state to which England would be reduced if the public debt were allowed to expand indefinitely: "No expedient at all remains for resisting tyranny: Elections are swayed by bribery and corruption alone: And the middle power between king and people being totally removed, a grievous despotism must infallibly prevail" (p. 99). Hume and Montesquieu corresponded on these matters; see the excerpts reprinted in *Writings on Economics*, p. 189.

and reason. This sort of discourse convinces every-body, but changes nobody. . . . I believe it is better to follow a roundabout road and to try to convey to the great a distaste [for the passions] by showing how little they yield that is at all useful.[8]

Montesquieu was thus motivated by his central polit-ical principles to ferret out, to welcome, and also to exaggerate the beneficial political effects that might flow from the bill of exchange and foreign exchange arbitrage. These institutions and operations accord well with the political concern that animates the major part of his work: to discover a means of checking the abuse of unlimited power. His advocacy of the separation of powers and of mixed government arose from his search for countervailing power; for, in spite of radically differ-ent conclusions, he agreed with Hobbes that "every man who has power tends to abuse that power; he will go up to the point where he meets with barriers."[9] In his note-book he had copied an English phrase he had read in 1730, during his sojourn in England, in *The Craftsman*, Bolingbroke's critical periodical:

The love of power is natural; it is insatiable; almost constantly whetted, and never cloyed by possession.[d]

And, as a result, he conceived of the principle of separa-tion of powers and of various other devices because, as he says in a famous phrase,

d *Oeuvres complètes*, Vol. II, p. 1358. In tracing the influences on Montesquieu's political doctrine, Robert Shackleton sees great significance in the fact that Montesquieu, "although he had some difficulty in copying out words in a foreign language, reproduced in his scrapbook, in his own hand, the arguments of the danger attached to power." "Montesquieu, Bolingbroke, and the Separa-tion of Powers," *French Studies* 3 (1949), p. 37.

So that there may be no abuse of power, it is necessary that, through the disposition of things (*par
la disposition des choses*), power be stopped by
power.[10]

The appropriate *disposition des choses* that will restrain the otherwise ceaseless expansion of power is to
be achieved primarily by building various institutional
and constitutional safeguards into the political system.
But why not include into that *disposition* anything else
that may be helpful? When he came to discuss economic
matters Montesquieu perceived, as noted above, that
the desire for gain is self-propelling and insatiable, just
like the drive for power. But although he viewed the
latter with grave concern, we know that he saw nothing
but *douceur* in the former. Hence it was only natural
that he should have looked out for specific ways in which
the acquisitive urge could be incorporated into the
proper *disposition des choses*. In the key sentence of
page 73, above, where the passions of the sovereign are
viewed as being tamed by his interests, he performed a
junction and fusion of prevailing contemporary notions
about countervailing passion with his own theory of
countervailing power. He hailed the bill of exchange
and arbitrage as auxiliaries of the constitutional safeguards and as bulwarks against despotism and *les grands
coups d'autorité*; and there can be little doubt that these
passages on the favorable political consequences of economic expansion constitute an important, and hitherto
neglected, contribution to his central political thesis,
just as they represent a basic justification of the new
commercial-industrial age.

As presented so far, the doctrine of Montesquieu is

entirely concerned with domestic governance and politics. This was indeed the principal concern of political thought, the traditional arena in which proposals for reform through institutional-constitutional engineering were put forward. Nevertheless, in the seventeenth and eighteenth centuries there was increasing concern over international relations and, in particular, over the virtually permanent state of war in which the major powers were embroiled. To the extent that war was thought to be due to the passionate and willful excesses of the rulers, any improvement in domestic political or economic organization that would effectively curb such behavior would of course indirectly have beneficial international consequences and enhance the chances for peace. But international commerce, being a transaction between nations, could conceivably have also a direct impact on the likelihood of peace and war: once again the interests might overcome the passions, specifically the passion for conquest. Because of the comparatively underdeveloped state of thinking on international relations, speculations of this sort were generally formulated in vague generalities and unsupported pronouncements.

Actually the general opinion on the effect of commerce on international discord or harmony changed substantially from the seventeenth to the eighteenth century. Whether because of mercantilist doctrine or because of the fact that markets were in fact so limited that an expansion of the commerce of one nation could only be secured by displacing that of another, commerce was characterized as "perpetual combat" by Colbert and as "a kind of warfare" by Sir Josiah Child.[11] Basic conditions and doctrines under which commerce was carried on were substantially unchanged some fifty years later.

Nevertheless, Jean-François Melon, a close friend of Montesquieu, proclaims in 1734:

> The spirit of conquest and the spirit of commerce are mutually exclusive in a nation.[12]

Montesquieu affirms just as categorically:

> the natural effect of commerce is to lead to peace. Two nations that trade together become mutually dependent: if one has an interest in buying, the other has one in selling; and all unions are based on mutual needs.[13]

This dramatic change in opinion about the effect of commerce on peace may be related to Montesquieu's thought on the domestic political consequences of economic expansion. It was difficult to maintain that domestically such expansion would lead to constraints on the behavior of the rulers while internationally it would cause wars when these were increasingly viewed as motivated by dynastic ambition and folly (as in *Candide*) rather than by "true interest."

Actually Montesquieu's praise for commerce was not without reservations. In the same chapter in which he commends commerce for its contribution to peace, he regrets the way in which commerce brings with it a monetization of all human relations and the loss of hospitality and of other "moral virtues which lead one to not always discuss one's interests with rigidity."[14]

Melon has no such qualms. On the contrary, he wishes to reassure those who might fear that commerce, in bringing peace and tranquility, would cause the loss of qualities such as courage and daring. He affirms that these qualities would not only survive but flourish because of the perils of navigation that seaborne trade continually faces.[15] Thus everything is truly for the best: commerce acts, at one and the same time, as a preventive of war and as a moral equivalent for it!

2. SIR JAMES STEUART

Set against the backdrop of a country where, in mid-eighteenth century, no clear remedy against disastrously arbitrary rule was in sight, Montesquieu's partial reliance on commerce, the bill of exchange, and arbitrage as safeguards against *les grands coups d'autorité* and war can be interpreted as a counsel of despair or, alternatively, as an extraordinary leap of optimistic imagination. In England there was less need to look so far afield, the power of the Crown being anything but absolute by the eighteenth century. Nevertheless, similar ideas crop up among the political economists and historical sociologists of the "Scottish Enlightenment" in the second half of the century.

For such figures as Adam Smith, Adam Ferguson, and John Millar, these ideas probably sprang from their common conviction that economic changes are the basic determinants of social and political transformation.[16] But for Sir James Steuart, who presented ideas similar to those of Montesquieu in the most explicit and general form, the explanation is even simpler: his major work, the *Inquiry into the Principles of Political Oeconomy* (1767), was largely conceived and written during his long exile from England on the European Continent where the interrelation between political conditions and economic progress was particularly obvious. Moreover, the influence of Montesquieu's thought is evident throughout his work, with respect to both general principles and numerous specific points of analysis.

For example, Montesquieu's ideas on the political effects of the bill of exchange and of arbitrage are distinctly echoed in the chapter in which Steuart describes "The general Consequences resulting to a trading Nation upon the opening of an active foreign Commerce" in the following terms:

> The statesman looks about with amazement; he who was wont to consider himself as the first man in the society in every respect, perceives himself eclipsed by the lustre of private wealth, *which avoids his grasp when he attempts to seize it.* This makes his government more complex and more difficult to be carried on; *he must now avail himself of art and address* as well as of power and authority.[17]

The same idea is expressed again when Steuart says that "the monied interest," in contrast to the landlords with their "solid property," "can baffle [the statesman's] attempts" and can frustrate "his schemes of laying hold of private wealth."[18]

This thought about the expansion-induced constraints on the grasping authority and arbitrary exactions of the political power holders is elaborated and presented in more general form when the social and political consequences of economic expansion—he calls it "the establishment of trade and industry"—are specifically examined later in the same chapter.

As in the previously cited passage, Steuart shows himself to be uniquely aware of a remarkable puzzle. Thoroughly familiar with mercantilist thinking and in some respects still under its influence, he knew that trade and industry, if conducted properly, were supposed to increase the power of the realm and therefore that of the sovereign. At the same time, observation of *actual* social development as well as, presumably, acquaintance with the new historical thought of his fellow Scots, such as David Hume and William Robertson, pointed to a very different set of consequences: trade expansion strengthened the position of the "middle rank of men" at the expense of the lords and eventually also of the king. Standing at the crossroads of these two contradictory analyses or conjectures, Steuart boldly reconciled them by one of those dialectical sequences which, together with other indications, makes it likely that his thought had an influence on Hegel.[19] He maintains, in true mercantilist fashion, that the "introduction of trade and industry" originates in the statesman's ambition to gain power, but then shows how things take a rather unexpected turn:

> Trade and industry . . . owed their establishment to the ambition of princes . . . principally with a view to enrich themselves, and thereby to become formidable to their neighbours. But they did not discover, until experience taught them, that the wealth they drew from such fountains was but the overflowing of the spring; and that an opulent, bold, and spirited people, having the fund of the prince's wealth in their own hands, have it also in their own power, when it becomes strongly their inclination, to shake off his authority. The consequence of this change has been the introduction of a more mild, and a more regular plan of administration.

> When once a state begins to subsist by the consequences of industry, there is less danger to be apprehended from the power of the sovereign. The mechanism of his administration becomes more complex, and . . . he finds himself so bound up by

the laws of his political oeconomy, that every transgression of them runs him into new difficulties.

At this point Steuart hedges a bit:

> I speak of governments only which are conducted
> systematically, constitutionally, and by general laws;
> and when I mention princes, I mean their councils.
> The principles I am enquiring into, regard the cool
> administration of their government; it belongs to
> another branch of politics, to contrive bulwarks
> against their passions, vices and weaknesses, as
> men.[20]

But he forgets all about this caution when he returns,
a few chapters later, to the topic of the "restrictions"
that the "complicated system of modern oeconomy" entails for the conduct of public affairs. He makes again a
two-sided point: on the one hand, increasing wealth
causes the statesman to have "so powerful an influence
over the operations of a whole people . . . which in former ages, even under the most absolute governments
was utterly unknown"; at the same time, however, "the
sovereign power is extremely limited, in every *arbitrary*
exercise of it" (Steuart's emphasis). The reason lies in
the nature of the "complicated modern oeconomy,"
which he also calls "the plan" or "the plan of oeconomy":

> . . . the execution of the plan will prove absolutely
> inconsistent with every arbitrary or irregular meas-
> ure.

> The power of a modern prince, let it be, by the
> constitution of his kingdom, ever so absolute, im-
> mediately becomes limited so soon as he establishes
> the plan of oeconomy which we are endeavouring
> to explain. If his authority formerly resembled the
> solidity and force of the wedge (which may indiffer-

ently be made use of, for splitting of timber, stones and other hard bodies, and which may be thrown aside and taken up again at pleasure), it will at length come to resemble the delicacy of the watch, which is good for no other purpose than to mark the progression of time, and which is immediately destroyed, if put to any other use, or touched with any but the gentlest hand.

[A] modern oeconomy, therefore, is the most effectual bridle ever was invented against the folly of despotism. . . .[21]

Here is another spectacular formulation of the idea originally framed by Montesquieu, that owing to the "complicated system of modern oeconomy" the interests would win out over arbitrary government, over the "folly of despotism," in short, over the passions of the rulers. This time Steuart throws his earlier caution to the winds and clearly sees expanding commerce and industry as reliable "bulwarks against [men's] passions, vices, and weaknesses."

As with Montesquieu, the set of ideas singled out here is better appreciated if they are related to the rest of Steuart's thought. For Montesquieu, it was not difficult to show that his speculations on the political implications of commercial expansion fit in quite closely with the leading themes of his work. But, with Steuart, one's first reaction is the imputation of inconsistency: the *Inquiry* has long been known as a book in which the "statesman"[e] is constantly steering things in one direction or another to keep the economy on an even course,

---

[e] This is Steuart's shorthand expression "to signify the legislature or supreme power, according to the form of government." *Inquiry*, Vol. I, p. 16. In general, however, Steuart uses the term with the meaning of an enlightened or to-be-enlightened policy maker interested only in the public good.

and attempts at rehabilitating Steuart as a great econo-
mist have shown him as a predecessor of Malthus,
Keynes, and of the "economics of control."[22] How is it
possible, then, that he should have argued at the same
time that the "introduction of modern oeconomy"
would *restrict* or *constrain* the statesman to a previously
unheard-of extent?

The explanation lies in the distinction, implicit in
Steuart, between "arbitrary" abuses of power that stem
from the vices and passions of the rulers (and that are
closely related to Montesquieu's *grands coups d'autorité*),
on the one hand, and the "fine tuning" carried out by
a hypothetical statesman exclusively motivated by the
common good, on the other.[f] According to Steuart, modern economic expansion puts an end to the former type
of intervention, but then creates a special need for the
latter kind if the economy is to move along a reasonably
smooth trajectory.

The basic consistency of Steuart's thinking is best
understood through his metaphor of the watch to which
he likens the "modern oeconomy." He uses it on two
different occasions to illustrate in turn the two aspects
of state intervention that have just been mentioned.
On the one hand, the watch is so delicate that it "is immediately destroyed if . . . touched with any but the
gentlest hand"[23]; this means that the penalty for old-
fashioned arbitrary *coups d'autorité* is so stiff that they
will simply have to cease. On the other hand, these same
watches "are continually going wrong; sometimes the
spring is found too weak, at other times too strong for
the machine . . . and the workman's hand becomes nec-

---

[f] The most general assumption of Steuart throughout his book
is that individuals are motivated by their self-interest, whereas
"public spirit . . . ought to be all-powerful in the statesman."
Inquiry, Vol. I, pp. 142–143. See also above, pp. 49–50.

essary to set it right"[24]; hence well-intentioned, delicate interventions are frequently required.

One cannot help thinking here of the metaphor likening the universe to a clock that was constantly used in the seventeenth and eighteenth centuries.[25] Its corollary was that God was made to change professions or "retool": from the potter He had been in the Old Testament, He now became a master clockmaker, *le Grand Horloger*. The implication was of course that once He had built the clock, it was going to run entirely by itself. Steuart's watch (= economy) shares with the clock (= universe) the quality of being a finely built mechanism that should not be tampered with by arbitrary outside interference, but by choosing the image of a watch he manages to convey both the impossibility of arbitrary and careless handling and the need for frequent corrective moves by the solicitous and expert "statesman."

3. JOHN MILLAR

Montesquieu and Steuart both believed that the expansion of commerce and industry would eliminate arbitrary and authoritarian decisionmaking by the sovereign. Their reasoning is similar, if not identical. Montesquieu generalizes from situations in which the state is largely deprived, as a result of the rise of specific new financial institutions, of its traditional power to seize property and to debase the currency at will. For Steuart, it is rather the overall complexity and vulnerability of the "modern oeconomy" that make arbitrary decisions and interferences unthinkable—that is, exorbitantly costly and disruptive.

In both situations, then, the sovereign is prevented or deterred from acting as violently or unpredictably as before, even though he may still very well wish to do so. The Montesquieu-Steuart position relies more on constraining, inhibiting, and sanctioning the prince than on motivating him to contribute directly to the nation's prosperity—a course advocated by the Physiocrats, as will be noted shortly.

The "deterrence model" chosen by Montesquieu and Steuart, particularly the variant put forward by the latter, stood in need of further elaboration. After all, deterrence may fail and the prince may decide to have his fling or *grand coup d'autorité* anyway. In that event the situation could still be saved if there were forces in the society that would rapidly mobilize to oppose the prince and make him retract or modify his policies. What was needed was a feedback or equilibrating mechanism that would restore conditions favorable to the expansion of commerce and industry should they be disturbed. Such a mechanism could be said to be implicit in the rise of the merchant and middle classes, as it was described by many eighteenth-century writers, from Hume to Adam Smith and Ferguson. An explicit account of the historical reasons for which these classes not only come to exercise increasing political influence in general but are able to *react* to abuses of power by others through collective action was put forward by John Millar, another prominent member of the Scottish Enlightenment.

In a posthumous essay entitled "The Advancement of Manufactures, Commerce, and the Arts; and the Tendency of this Advancement to diffuse a Spirit of Liberty and Independence," Millar states his principal subject as follows:

The spirit of liberty appears, in commercial countries, to depend chiefly upon two circumstances:

first, the condition of the people relative to the distribution of property, and the means of subsistence: secondly, the facility with which the several members of society are enabled to associate and to act in concert with one another.[26]

In accordance with this outline, he first shows how the advances of productivity in manufacturing and agriculture lead in both these branches to greater "personal independence, and to higher notions of general liberty." He also believes it likely that these advances will not be accompanied by the very great inequalities of fortune that were characteristic of the prior age, but by "such a gradation of opulence, as leaving no chasm from top to bottom of the scale."[27]

Having satisfied himself in this manner that the advance of commerce and manufactures gives rise to a general diffusion of the spirit of liberty, Millar points out more specifically how this advance enhances the ability of certain social groups to resort to collective action against oppression and mismanagement. Locke's right to rebel is here subjected to an engaging sociological analysis, which is worth quoting at length:

... when a set of magistrates, and rulers, are invested with an authority, confirmed by ancient usage, and supported, perhaps, by an armed force, it cannot be expected that the people, single and unconnected, will be able to resist the oppression of their governors; and their power of combining for this purpose, must depend very much upon their peculiar circumstances. . . . [I]n large kingdoms, the people being dispersed over a wide country, have seldom been capable of . . . vigorous exertions. Living in petty villages, at a distance from one another, and having very imperfect means of communication, they are often but little affected by the hardships which many of their countrymen may sustain from the tyranny of government; and a rebellion may be quelled in one quarter before it has time to break out in another. . . .

From the progress, however, of trade and manufactures, the state of a country, in this respect, is gradually changed. As the inhabitants multiply from the facility of procuring subsistence, they are collected in large bodies for the convenient exercise of their employments. Villages are enlarged into towns; and these are often swelled into populous cities. In all those places of resort, there arise large bands of labourers or artificers, who by following the same employment, and by constant intercourse, are enabled, with great rapidity, to communicate all their sentiments and passions. Among these there spring up leaders, who give a tone and direction to their companions. The strong encourage the feeble; the bold animate the timid; the resolute confirm the wavering; and the movements of the whole mass proceed *with the uniformity of a machine*, and with a force that is often irresistible.

In this situation, a great proportion of the people are easily roused by every popular discontent, and can unite with no less facility in demanding a redress of grievances. The least ground of complaint, in a town, becomes the occasion of a riot; and the flames of sedition spreading from one city to another, are blown up into a general insurrection.

Neither does this union arise merely from local situations; nor is it confined to the lower class of those who are subservient to commerce and manufactures. *By a constant attention to professional objects,* the superior orders of mercantile people become quick-sighted in discerning their common interest, and, at all times, indefatigable in pursuing it. While the farmer, employed in the separate cultivation of his land, considers only his own individual profit; while the landed gentleman seeks only to procure a revenue sufficient for the supply of his wants, and is often unmindful of his own interest as well as of every other; the merchant, though he never overlooks his private advantage, is accustomed to connect his own gain with that of his brethren, and is, therefore, always ready to join with those of the same profession, in soliciting the aid of government, and in promoting general measures for the benefit of their trade.

The prevalence of this great mercantile association in Britain, has, in the course of the present century, become gradually more and more conspicuous. The clamor and tumultuary proceedings of the populace in the great towns *are capable of penetrating the inmost recesses of administration, of intimidating the boldest minister, and of displacing the most presumptuous favourite of the backstairs. The voice of the mercantile interest never fails to command the attention of government,* and when firm and unanimous, is even able to control and direct the deliberations of the national councils.[28]

The most striking feature of these paragraphs is the positive view Millar takes of the social role of riots and other mass actions. A few decades later the climate had totally changed, as Dr. Andrew Ure attested in his *Philosophy of Manufactures* (1835):

> Manufactures naturally condense a vast population within a narrow circuit; they afford every facility for secret cabal . . .; they communicate intelligence and energy to the vulgar mind; they supply in their liberal wages the pecuniary sinews of contention.[29]

By 1835, of course, the frequently "contentious" working class had come into existence. The eighteenth century events on which Millar based his optimistic view of mass action are probably the Wilkes riots, which shook London intermittently in the sixties and seventies.[30] As Rudé has shown, these riots were characterized by that very alliance of the merchants and other middle-class elements with the "crowd" that is so well conveyed in Millar's account.[31] Nevertheless, other contemporary observers seem to have been fairly alarmed by these riots. They caused David Hume to turn much more conservative and to suppress, in a new edition of his *Essays*, an extensive optimistic appraisal of the prospects for liberty in which he had said, for example, "that the people are no such dangerous monster as they have been represented."[32] Millar's account is at times not so reassuring either (except to a revolutionary), particularly when he adumbrates the possibility of a "general insurrection"; but on the whole his emphasis is on the "constant attention to professional objects" by the merchants and on their superior ability, in comparison with the widely scattered farmers, to organize themselves for "interest group" action, to rally others to their cause, and to obtain redress of grievances from the wayward policy makers. In this manner the process described by Millar exhibits the "discriminating purposefulness" and "focused character" that appears to have been the hallmark of eighteenth-century mobs in Western Europe.[33] Just as these mobs were considered to have a "constitutional role" to play in England and even in colonial America,[34] so John Millar endowed them with a highly rational and beneficent role in maintaining and defending economic progress.

Moreover, just as Steuart had likened the working of the "modern oeconomy" to the "delicacy of a watch," the movements of the "mercantile people" and their allies are viewed here as proceeding "with the uniformity of a machine." Clearly Millar was convinced that he had uncovered an important and reliable mechanism that would insure that the passions of the prince could not prevail for long over the public interest and the needs of the expanding economy. In this sense his thought completes that of Montesquieu and Steuart.

Related yet Discordant Views

THE Montesquieu-Steuart view of the political consequences of economic expansion was by no means universally shared. In fact, the most influential writers on economic affairs in France and England, the Physiocrats and Adam Smith, not only failed to add to the specific line of thought that has been developed; as will be shown, they—particularly Adam Smith—contributed in various ways to its demise.

A number of important ideas and concerns are shared by the two groups, but emphasis and conclusions often differ markedly. For example, the idea of the economy as an intricately built mechanism or machine that functions independently of men's will was one of the most important contributions of the Physiocrats to economic thought.[35] In the course of his European wanderings Steuart had been in touch with several prominent members of that school,[36] and his view of the modern economy as a watch-like mechanism may have been influenced by their way of thinking. But the conclusion the Physiocrats drew from their insight was not to prognosticate, like Steuart, that nobody would dare interfere with the working of the machine but to advocate a political order in which interference would be effectively barred.

Similarly, the Physiocrats and Adam Smith shared with their contemporaries the belief in the importance of the distinction between movable and unmovable property. This distinction had first suggested the thought to Montesquieu that governments dealing with citizens owning primarily movable property will have to behave quite differently from those facing societies where unmovable property is the principal form of privately held wealth. In *The Wealth of Nations* this distinction and the ability of the holders of capital to remove themselves to another country are mentioned several times and are indeed recognized as restraints on extortionist tax policies.[37] But Adam Smith does not go further. In their basic text, *Philosophie rurale,* Quesnay and Mirabeau also point to the elusive character of wealth in commercial societies and come in fact quite close to the analysis of Montesquieu; but they do so in a very different spirit:

> All the possessions [of commercial societies] consisted of scattered and secret securities, a few warehouses, and passive and active debts, whose true

94

owners are to some extent unknown, since no one knows which of them are paid and which of them are owing. No wealth which is immaterial or kept in people's pockets can ever be got hold of by the sovereign power, and consequently will yield it nothing at all. This is a truth which should be constantly repeated to the governments of those agricultural nations which take such pains to school themselves to become merchants, i.e. to plunder themselves. The wealthy merchant, trader, banker, etc., will always be a member of a republic. In whatever place he may live, he will always enjoy the immunity which is inherent in the scattered and unknown character of his property, all one can see of which is the place where business in it is transacted. It would be useless for the authorities to try to force him to fulfill the duties of a subject: they are obliged, in order to induce him to fit in with their plans, to treat him as a master, and to make it worth his while to contribute voluntarily to the public revenue.[38]

Obviously Quesnay and Mirabeau feel, first of all, that the elusive qualities of commerce and industry are a liability rather than an asset and make it advisable for a country not to encourage these activities.[g] Secondly, they simply assume that wealthy merchants and bankers will somehow return to the medieval pattern and organize themselves in separate republics. Hence the problem of political organization in "agricultural societies"

[g] The fears and hopes aroused by the emergence of the various forms of *movable* capital as a major component of total wealth in the eighteenth century offer many interesting parallels with similarly contradictory perceptions caused more recently by the rise of the multinational corporation.

(among which France was implicitly included) remains unsolved.

Finally and most important, the two groups of writers are equally convinced that incompetent, arbitrary, and wasteful policies of the rulers can seriously impede economic progress. Some of Adam Smith's most eloquent pages denounce such policies,[39] and the following indictment by Quesnay can stand as a useful listing of the principal varieties of Montesquieu's *grands coups d'autorité*:

> . . . the despotism of the sovereigns and of their underlings, the shortcomings and the instability of the laws, the disorderly excesses (*dérèglements*) of the administration, the uncertainty affecting property, the wars, the chaotic decisions in matters of taxation destroy men and the wealth of the sovereign.[40]

But, once again, neither the Physiocrats nor Adam Smith were willing to rely on economic expansion to achieve the "withering away" of this sort of wrongheadedness on the part of the politicians. Rather, they advocated that these ills be dealt with directly: the Physiocrats came out in favor of a new political order that would ensure the correct economic policies as defined by them, while Adam Smith aimed more modestly at changing specific policies. We shall deal with their respective positions in turn.

1. THE PHYSIOCRATS

On the question of political organization, comparatively small differences in approach led Montesquieu and the Physiocrats to take perfectly opposite stands.

Montesquieu set out to design political and economic institutions that would effectively restrain the passionate excesses of the sovereign. The Physiocrats were just a little more ambitious: they wanted to motivate him to act correctly (that is, in accordance with Physiocrat doctrine) of his own free will. In other words, they were looking for a political order in which the power holders are impelled, *for reasons of self-interest,* to promote the general interest. The quest for this particular harmony of interests had been Hobbes's way of posing the problem of the best form of government, and it had led him to favor absolute monarchy over democracy and aristocracy:

> . . . where the publique and private interest [of the ruler] are most closely united there is the publique most advanced. Now in Monarchy, the private interest is the same with the publique. The riches, power, and honour of a Monarch arise only from the riches, strength and reputation of his Subjects. For no King can be rich, nor glorious, nor secure; whose Subjects are either poore, contemptible, or too weak through want, or dissention, to maintain a war against their enemies: Whereas in a Democracy, or Aristocracy, the publique prosperity conferres not so much to the private fortune of one that is corrupt, or ambitious, as doth many times a perfidious advice, a treacherous action, or a Civill warre.[41]

In their political writings the Physiocrats took over the same thought and had only sarcasm for Montesquieu's advocacy of a form of government that they saw as condemned to be weak and hobbled. At the same time, they formulated in the laissez-faire principle the other, better known harmony-of-interests doctrine according to which the public good is the outcome of the free pursuit by everyone of his own self-interest. Being located at the intersection of these two *Harmonielehren*, the Physiocrats oddly advocate both freedom from governmental interference with the market and the enforcement of this freedom by an all-powerful ruler whose self-interest is tied up with the "right" economic system. The latter arrangement is referred to by them as "legal despotism," which they oppose to the "arbitrary despotism" that is guilty of the misdeeds so well detailed by Quesnay.[42]

Going further than Hobbes, who relied on the general convergence of interests between the Many and the One who rules, some of the Physiocrats invented institutional arrangements specifically designed to make the despot truly "legal." On the one hand, they elaborated a system of judicial control that would see to it that the laws issued by the sovereign and his council are not contrary to the "natural order" that is to be reflected in the fundamental constitution of the state.[43] But an even more important safeguard was the idea that the sovereign should be given a real stake in the prosperity of his commonwealth. This was the purpose of the institution of co-property that Le Mercier de la Rivière proposed in his *Ordre naturel et essentiel des sociétés politiques* (1767).[44] According to his plan, the sovereign would be co-owner, in a set and unchangeable proportion, of all the productive resources and of the *produit net*: as a result, any conflict of interests between him and the country at large would be inconceivable, and the Hobbesian identity of interests would be transparent even to the most obtuse and wicked despot.

It was Linguet, eternal *enfant terrible* and a critic of both Montesquieu and the Physiocrats, who carried this manner of reasoning to its ultimate conclusion. Logically enough, he felt that a co-property arrangement with the monarch would not be quite sufficient as an assurance of the sought-after identity of interests; so he went one step further and came out in favor of *total* ownership of all national wealth by the ruler. With great consistency he praises "oriental" or "Asian despotism" and concludes that the system he advocates

does not at all favor tyranny contrary to what many think; it imposes on the kings obligations that are much narrower than the so-called dependence in which some would like to place them in relation to their own vassals. [This ideal system] does not only advise them to be just; it forces them to be so.[45]

This passage is strongly reminiscent of Steuart's phrase about the "folly of despotism" becoming impossible with "modern oeconomy." The crucial difference of course is that the Physiocrats (as well as Linguet) expected their ideal system of political economy to be enacted by enlightened statesmen, as a result of the persuasiveness of their arguments;[46] whereas Sir James Steuart thought that change in the desired direction would occur of its own accord, as a result of the ongoing process of economic expansion.

It is not too difficult to conceive of a position that partakes of both these points of view: Marxism has in fact thoroughly habituated us to the possibility of believing at one and the same time that historical forces move inexorably toward a certain outcome *and* that those who wish for that outcome had better devote all their energy to bringing it about. Actually every policy-oriented writer in the social sciences faces the problem of the proper mix between prediction and prescription, and it is now time to take a look at the very complex position taken in this respect by Adam Smith.

2. ADAM SMITH AND THE END OF A VISION

The main impact of *The Wealth of Nations* was to establish a powerful *economic* justification for the un-trammeled pursuit of individual self-interest, whereas in the earlier literature that has been surveyed here the stress was on the *political* effects of this pursuit. But no attentive reader of *Wealth* will be surprised that arguments of the latter kind can also be found in that protean volume. Actually Adam Smith presents at one point the idea that increase in wealth and retrenchment in power go hand in hand, and he does so at greater length and with more relish than any other writer had done up to his time. The place is his well-known account of the erosion of feudalism in Chapter 4 of Book III, entitled "How the Commerce of Towns Contributed to the Improvement of the Country." Here Smith sets out to tell the story how

> commerce and manufactures gradually introduced order and good government, and with them, the liberty and security of individuals, among the inhabitants of the country, who had before lived almost in a continual state of war with their neighbours, and of servile dependency upon their superiors.[47]

The story can be retold succinctly, and to convey the correct flavor I shall use, as much as possible, Adam

Smith's own brilliantly caustic words.[h] Before the rise of commerce and industry, the great lords shared the surplus from their estates with large numbers of retainers, who were wholly dependent on the lords and constituted a private army, as well as with their tenants, who paid low rents but had no security of tenure. This state of affairs resulted in a situation in which "the king was . . . incapable of restraining the violence of the great lords. . . . They [made] war according to their own discretion, almost continually upon one another, and very frequently upon the king; and the open country . . . [was] a scene of violence, rapine, and disorder."[48]

But then matters changed as a result of "the silent and insensible operation of foreign commerce and manufactures." The lords now had something on which they could spend their surplus, which they had previously shared with their retainers and tenants: "a pair of diamond buckles, or . . . something as frivolous and useless," "trinkets and baubles, fitter to be the playthings of children than the serious pursuits of man," is the contemptuous way in which Adam Smith refers to the merchandise offered by the townsmen. This merchandise was so attractive to the lords that they decided to do without retainers and to enter into longer-term and generally more businesslike relations with their tenants. In the upshot, "for the gratification of the most childish, the meanest and the most sordid of all vanities they gradually bartered their whole power and authority"[49] and "became as insignificant as any substantial burgher or tradesman in a city."[50] And the grand political result was that

[h] It is a mystery how Schumpeter could have qualified the "wisdom" of Book III as "dry and uninspired." See his *History of Economic Analysis* (New York: Oxford University Press, 1954), p. 187.

... the great proprietors were no longer capable of interrupting the regular execution of justice, or of disturbing the peace of the country.[51]

Once again, then, the rise of commerce and industry makes for more orderly government, but the modus operandi is very different from that invoked by Montesquieu and Steuart. In the first place, the latter were concerned with the supreme authority of the king, its uses and abuses, whereas Smith addressed himself to the overweening power of the feudal lords. Secondly, he saw a decline in this power, not because the lords came to realize that their interest lay in not using it so wantonly as before, but because they *unwittingly* relinquished their power as they attempted to take advantage of the new opportunities for their own consumption and material improvement opened up by the "progress of the arts." In fact, the episode is better summarized as a victory of the passions (of cupidity and luxury) over the longer-run interests of the lords than as the taming of the passions by the interests.

The form of the argument Adam Smith chose made it difficult to extend it from the lords to the sovereign. In Hume's *History of England*, which Smith quotes at the outset of his own story, the rise of the "middle rank of men" had been set forth in rather similar, if considerably less colorful, terms; and Hume specifically pointed out that the loss of power of the lords benefited not only the newly rising merchants and manufacturers but the sovereign as well, and Adam Smith himself had used a similar argument in the *Lectures*.[52] With respect to arbitrary decisions and harmful policies of the *central* government, Smith does not hold out much hope that economic development itself will bring improvements.

At one point, when speaking about "the capricious ambition of kings and ministers," he says specifically:

> The violence and injustice of the rulers of mankind is an ancient evil, for which, I am afraid, the nature of human affairs can scarce admit of a remedy.[53]

And in a polemic with Quesnay he maintains that considerable economic progress is possible regardless of improvements in the political environment:

> . . . in the political body, the natural effort which every man is continually making to better his own condition, is a principle of preservation capable of preventing and correcting, in many respects, the bad effects of a political economy, in some degree both partial and oppressive . . . . [T]he wisdom of nature has fortunately made ample provisions for remedying many of the bad effects of the folly and injustice of man. . . .[54]

He uses very similar terms in his "Digression on the Corn Trade":

> The natural effort of every individual to better his own condition, when suffered to exert itself with freedom and security, is so powerful a principle, that it is alone, and without any assistance, not only capable of carrying on the society to wealth and prosperity, but of surmounting a hundred impertinent obstructions with which the folly of human laws too often encumbers its operations.[55]

Smith affirms here that economics can go it alone: within wide limits of tolerance, political progress is not needed as a prerequisite for, nor is it likely to be a consequence of, economic advance, at least at the level of the highest councils of government.[i] In this view, very different from the laissez-faire or minimal state doctrine and still widespread today among economists, politics is the province of the "folly of men" while economic progress, like Candide's garden, can be cultivated with success provided such folly does not exceed some fairly ample and flexible limits. It appears that Smith advocated less a state with minimal functions than one whose capacity for folly would have some ceiling.

Adam Smith did not share the Montesquieu-Steuart perspective for a number of other, still more important reasons. For one, to the extent that he felt strongly about specific aspects of governmental "folly" which did, in his opinion, hold back economic advance (such as certain mercantilist policies), he was intent, like the Physiocrats, on describing these policies as hard realities that had to be changed rather than on discovering grounds for hope that they would dissolve of their own accord.

Secondly, Smith was not nearly so ready as Montesquieu and Steuart to hail the new era of trade and industry as one that would deliver mankind from ancient evils, such as abuses of power, wars, and the like. His

[i] On this point, as well as elsewhere in the next few pages, my interpretation differs strongly from that presented by Joseph Cropsey in his thought-provoking essay *Polity and Economy: An Interpretation of the Principles of Adam Smith* (The Hague: Nijhoff, 1957). I shall simply state and document my point of view rather than compare it throughout with that of Cropsey, which "stated most generally" is that "Smith's position may be interpreted to mean that commerce generates freedom and civilization, and at the same time free institutions are indispensable to the preservation of commerce" (p. 95). A recent critical appraisal of Cropsey's interpretation is in Duncan Forbes, "Sceptical Whiggism, Commerce and Liberty" in A. S. Skinner and T. Wilson, eds., *Essays on Adam Smith* (New York: Oxford University Press, 1976), pp. 194–201.

well-known ambivalence toward material progress is in fact well illustrated in the manner of the historical account that has just been reported. While he obviously welcomed the outcome of the process he described—it was, after all, "order and good government, and with them, the liberty and security of individuals"—he was at the same time extraordinarily scathing with regard to the chain of events and the motivations that brought about this happy result. The explanation for this ambivalent stance may lie, at least in part, in the delight he took, here as elsewhere, in uncovering and emphasizing the unintended results of human action. One cannot help feeling that in this particular instance Smith overplayed his Invisible Hand: for the derisive and even savage manner of the account he gives of the "folly" of the lords raises the question in the reader's mind how the lords could have been quite so blind to their class interests.[j]

Smith's ambivalence toward nascent capitalism was not limited to this instance. Its most famous manifestation is perhaps his treatment of the division of labor, which he celebrates in Book I, only to castigate it in Book V. Much has been written about this contrast.[56] Here it is of particular interest that Smith sees the loss of the martial spirit and virtues as one of the *unfortunate* consequences of both the division of labor and of com-

---

[j] Both Hume, in the *History of England* (1762), and John Millar, in *The Origins of the Distinction of Ranks* (1771), also traced the loss of power of the lords to economic causes but gave more importance than Adam Smith to the new position of the "middle rank of men" who dealt with a large number of customers instead of being dependent on the favors of a single person. For John Millar's essay, see William C. Lehmann, *John Millar of Glasgow* (Cambridge: University Press, 1960), pp. 290–291; for Hume, see below, note 52 of Part Two.

merce in general. In relation to the former he says in
The Wealth of Nations about "the man whose whole life
is spent in performing a few simple operations":

> Of the great and extensive interests of his country
> he is altogether incapable of judging; and unless
> very particular pains have been taken to render him
> otherwise, he is equally incapable of defending his
> country in war. The uniformity of his stationary
> life naturally corrupts the courage of his mind, and
> makes him regard with abhorrence the irregular,
> uncertain, and adventurous life of a soldier.[57]

In the *Lectures* he had made the same point in relation
to commerce, totally espousing the classical "republican"
view that commerce leads to debilitating luxury and corruption.

> Another bad effect of commerce is that it sinks the
> courage of mankind, and tends to extinguish mar-
> tial spirit. . . . A man has . . . time to study only one
> branch of business, and it would be a great disad-
> vantage to oblige every one to learn the military art
> and to keep himself in the practice of it. The de-
> fence of the country is therefore committed to a cer-
> tain set of men who have nothing else ado, and
> among the bulk of the people military courage di-
> minishes. By having their minds constantly em-
> ployed on the arts of luxury, they grow effeminate
> and dastardly.[58]

In the summary of this section he repeats:

> These are the disadvantages of a commercial spirit.
> The minds of men are contracted, and rendered in-
> capable of elevation. Education is despised, or at

least neglected, and the heroic spirit is almost utterly extinguished. To remedy these defects would
be an object worthy of serious attention.[59]

These passages yield a rather straightforward explanation for Smith's failure to make much of the human and
political effects of the rise of commerce and industry:
while he saw some advantages to this rise, such as the
positive effect on probity and punctuality,[60] he perceived
as damaging some of the very consequences of commerce
that were hailed by writers such as Montesquieu who
had become more impressed by the disasters that the
"martial spirit" entails in the modern age. The *douceur*
that was celebrated by Montesquieu and others meant
corruption and decadence not only to Rousseau but to
some extent also to Smith. A full-blown expression of
this point of view can be found in the work of his fellow
Scot, Adam Ferguson, who retained ties with the "rude"
society of Scotland and whose *Essay on the History of
Civil Society* (1767) abounds with reservations about
the "polished" society of expanding commerce exhibited
by England.[61]

But Adam Smith's major impact on the ideas under
discussion lies still elsewhere. Not only did he not share,
in the various respects just noted, the Montesquieu-
Steuart perspective on the ability of emergent capitalism to improve the political order through control of
the wilder passions; he decisively undercut it and, in a
sense, gave it the *coup de grâce*. In his most important
and influential work Smith sees men actuated entirely
by the "desire of bettering [their] condition," and he
further specifies that "an augmentation of fortune is the
means by which the greater part of men propose and
wish to better their condition."[62] There seems to be no

place here for the richer concept of human nature in which men are driven by, and often torn between, diverse passions of which "avarice" was only one. Smith was of course fully aware of these other passions and had indeed devoted an important treatise to them. But it is precisely in *The Theory of Moral Sentiments* that he paves the way for collapsing these other passions into the drive for the "augmentation of fortune." Interestingly enough, he does so in the guise of doing the opposite; for he goes out of his way to stress the noneconomic and nonconsumptionist motives that are behind the struggle for economic advance. Since, as he says repeatedly, man's bodily needs are strictly limited,

> . . . it is chiefly from [the] regard to the sentiments of mankind that we pursue riches and avoid poverty. For to what purpose is all the toil and bustle of this world? What is the end of avarice and ambition, of the pursuit of wealth, of power and preeminence? . . . From whence . . . arises the emulation which runs through all the different ranks of men and what are the advantages which we propose by that great purpose of human life which we call *bettering our condition*? To be observed, to be attended to, to be taken notice of with sympathy, complacency, and appreciation, are all the advantages which we can propose to derive from it. It is the vanity, not the ease or the pleasure, which interests us.[63]

Much as in Hobbes and other seventeenth-century writers, the craving for honor, dignity, respect, and recognition is seen here as a basic preoccupation of man. But, as will be seen shortly, Hobbes had kept that crav-

ing separate from the "caring for necessary things."
More explicitly, Rousseau had made a fundamental and
famous distinction between *amour de soi,* which aims
at the satisfaction of our "real needs" through the acquisition of a finite amount of goods, and *amour propre,*
which is keyed to approval and admiration from our
fellow men and which by definition has no limit.[64] Thus
he says: "it is easy to see that all our labors are directed
upon two objects only, namely, the commodities of life
for oneself, and consideration on the part of others."[65]

This arrangement of all human "labors," that is,
drives and passions, into just two categories already
represents simplification on a grand scale. In the passage of *The Theory of Moral Sentiments* that was cited
above, Adam Smith then takes the final reductionist
step of turning two into one: the drive for economic
advantage is no longer autonomous but becomes a mere
vehicle for the desire for consideration. By the same
token, however, the noneconomic drives, powerful as
they are, are all made to feed into the economic ones
and do nothing but reinforce them, being thus deprived
of their erstwhile independent existence.

Two consequences follow. First, the solution to the
celebrated *Adam Smith Problem*—that is, to the puzzle
over the compatibility of *The Theory of Moral Sentiments* with *The Wealth of Nations*—may lie here. In
the former work, so it appears, Smith dealt with a wide
spectrum of human feelings and passions, but he also
convinced himself that, insofar as "the great mob of
mankind" is concerned, the principal human drives end
up motivating man to improve his material well-being.
And, logically enough, he then proceeded in *The
Wealth of Nations* to investigate in detail the conditions

under which this objective on which human action tends to converge so remarkably can be achieved. As a result of his emphasis on the noneconomic springs of economic action, it became possible for Smith to concentrate on economic behavior in a manner that was perfectly consistent with his earlier interest in other important dimensions of the human personality.

The second conclusion is more important from the point of view of the story that is being told here. By holding that ambition, the lust for power, and the desire for respect can all be satisfied by economic improvement, Smith undercut the idea that passion can be pitted against passion, or the interests against the passions. This whole train of thought becomes suddenly incomprehensible, if not nonsensical, and there is a return to the stage, prior to Bacon, when the major passions were considered to be a solid bloc and to feed on each other.[k] Small wonder, then, that Smith himself virtually equates the passions with the interests in a key passage of *The Wealth of Nations* where the modus operandi of the market society is described:

> It is thus that the private *interests and passions* of individuals naturally dispose them to turn their stock towards the employments which in ordinary cases are most advantageous to the society. But if from this natural preference they should turn too much of it towards those employments, the fall of profit in them and the rise of it in all others immediately dispose them to alter this faulty distribution. Without any intervention of law, therefore, *the private interests and passions* of men naturally lead them to divide and distribute the stock of every

[k] See above, p. 20.

society, among all the different employments carried on in it, as nearly as possible in the proportion
which is most agreeable to the interest of the whole
society.[66]

The two terms "interests" and "passions," which had
so frequently been antonyms in the century and a half
that had elapsed since the Duke of Rohan wrote *On the
Interest of Princes and States of Christendom*, appear
here, twice in succession, as synonyms. Although it
would be farfetched to see anything conscious or inten-
tional about it, the effect of this choice of language was
nevertheless to obliterate the rationale for reliance on
self-interest that was based on the opposition of the interests and the passions and on the ability of the former
to tame the latter. The paragraph just cited enthroned
Smith's own rationale, namely, the idea that the material
welfare of "the whole society" is advanced when everyone is allowed to follow his own private interest; at the
same time, his use of language destroyed in passing the
competing rationale.

One reason for which the passions came to be used
here as a redundant synonym of the interests is that
Adam Smith was concerned, far more than earlier writers, with the "great mob of mankind," that is, with the
average person and his behavior. According to a long
tradition, it was primarily the aristocracy that is animated by numerous noble or ignoble passions which
clash with the dictates of duty and reason or with one another. Machiavelli, in speaking about the prince, had considered it axiomatic that "his own passions . . . are much
greater than those of the people."[67] Or, as Hobbes
put it: "All men naturally strive for honour and preferment; but chiefly they, who are least troubled with

caring for necessary things" and "who otherwise live at ease, without fear of want."[68] Precisely for this reason, only members of present or past aristocracies were considered fit to appear as key figures in tragedies and other forms of "high" literature that typically dealt with the passions and the conflicts arising out of them.[69] The ordinary mortal was not thought to be so complicated. His principal concern was with subsistence and material improvement, generally as ends in themselves, and at best as proxies for the achievement of respect and admiration. Hence either he had no passions or his passions could be satisfied through the pursuit of his interests.

For those various reasons, then, *The Wealth of Nations* marks an end to the speculations about the effects of interest-motivated on passionate behavior that had exercised the minds of some of Smith's more illustrious predecessors. Attention of both scholarly and policy debate came to center after Smith on his proposition that the general (material) welfare is best served by letting each member of society pursue his own (material) self-interest. The success this proposition had in eclipsing the older problem can be explained, first of all, in terms of intellectual history. Even though Smith was careful to avoid and disavow the paradoxical manner with which Mandeville had put forth similar thoughts, his proposition still turned out to be riddled with so many intellectual puzzles that sorting and solving them occupied generations of economists. Moreover, the proposition and ensuing doctrine fulfilled another requirement of the highly successful paradigm: while it was a splendid generalization, it represented a considerable *narrowing* of the field of inquiry over which social thought had ranged freely up to then and thus permitted intellectual specialization and professionalization. But the disappearance from view of the Montesquieu-Steuart speculations must also be traced to more general historical factors: it is hardly surprising that their optimistic ideas on the political effects of expanding commerce and industry did not survive the age of the French Revolution and the Napoleonic Wars.

PART THREE

Reflections on an Episode
in Intellectual History

Where the Montesquieu-Steuart
Vision Went Wrong

I N AN old and well-known Jewish story, the rabbi of
Krakow interrupted his prayers one day with a wail
to announce that he had just seen the death of the rabbi
of Warsaw two hundred miles away. The Krakow con-
gregation, though saddened, was of course much impressed with the visionary powers of their rabbi. A few
days later some Jews from Krakow traveled to Warsaw
and, to their surprise, saw the old rabbi there officiate
in what seemed to be tolerable health. Upon their return they confided the news to the faithful and there was
incipient snickering. Then a few undaunted disciples
came to the defense of their rabbi; admitting that he
may have been wrong on the specifics, they exclaimed:
"Nevertheless, what vision!"

Ostensibly this story pours ridicule on the human
ability to rationalize belief in the face of contrary evidence. But at a deeper level it defends and celebrates
visionary and speculative thought no matter if such
thought goes astray. It is this interpretation that makes
the story so pertinent to the episode in intellectual
history that has been related here. The Montesquieu-
Steuart speculations about the salutary political consequences of economic expansion were a feat of imagination in the realm of political economy, a feat that
remains magnificent even though history may have
proven wrong the substance of those speculations.

Has it? The verdict on this question is not quite so
easy to reach as that on the nondeath of the Warsaw
rabbi. The century following the Napoleonic interlude
was, after all, comparatively peaceful and also witnessed

a decline in "despotism." But, as we all know, something went very much awry thereafter, and no twentieth-century observer can assert that the hopeful Montesquieu-Steuart vision has been triumphantly borne out by the course of events. It should nevertheless be remarked that the failure of the vision may well have been less than total. The forces observed by Montesquieu and Sir James Steuart could have asserted themselves, only to be overcome, perhaps narrowly, by others that worked in the opposite direction. Which, then, were the counterforces?

An inquiry into this question is likely to turn up connections between economic structures and political events that escaped the scrutiny of our two eighteenth-century visionaries and pioneers in political economy. A number of such connections were in fact soon noted by a few eighteenth- and nineteenth-century writers who continued the tradition of thought of the pioneers but added qualifications and provisos that, in effect, led to very different conclusions.

A brief survey of this kind of writing can begin with Joseph Barnave, the great orator of the Constituent Assembly of 1789–91 and author, just before his death under the guillotine, of an important interpretative essay in contemporary history, the *Introduction to the French Revolution*. While the emphasis of this work on social class has given Barnave some fame as a forerunner of Marxist thought, he viewed himself as an admirer and follower of Montesquieu. In a short paper on the "Effect of Commerce on Government" he indeed starts out much like the master:

> Commerce gives rise to a large class, disposed to external peace, internal tranquility, and attached to the established government.

118

But then comes a wholly different thought:

> The morals of a commercial nation are not com-
> pletely those of merchants. The merchant is thrifty;
> general morals are prodigal. The merchant main-
> tains his morals; public morals are dissolute.[1]

Just as Mandeville and Adam Smith had shown how
private individuals, by pursuing their vices or simply
their self-interest, could contribute to the social welfare,
so did Barnave argue here that what holds for the part
is not necessarily true for the whole. But this "fallacy of
composition"[a] is now invoked for the purpose of standing the earlier propositions on their head: Barnave proclaims that an aggregation of private *virtues* can result
in a state that is anything but virtuous. He does not
really explain why this should be so and asserts his
paradox only for the particular situation he is dealing
with. Nevertheless, he intimates persuasively that, because of the fallacy of composition, social processes are
much less transparent and amenable to prediction than
was confidently assumed by Montesquieu.

Barnave's procedure of first paying homage to the
conventional wisdom about the benign effect of commerce on society and politics and then bringing qualifications to bear on the argument is used in a more
devastating way by Adam Ferguson and later by
Tocqueville.

As a member of both a Scottish clan and the group of
thinkers who formed the Scottish Enlightenment, Ferguson was especially ambivalent about the advances
"polished" nations had achieved over the "rude and

---

[a] According to Paul A. Samuelson, the fallacy of composition
is one of the most basic and distinctive principles to be aware of
in the study of economics. See *Economics*, 3rd edn. (New York:
McGraw-Hill, 1955), p. 9.

barbarous" ones. Like Adam Smith, he noted the negative effects of the division of labor and commerce on the personality and social bonds of the individual citizen; but he emphasizes them right from the start of the *Essay on the History of Civil Society* (1767) and formulates his strictures at a more general level. In the process he anticipates not only the younger Marx but Durkheim and Tönnies as he contrasts the solidarity characteristic of closely knit tribes with the "spirit which reigns in a commercial state where . . . man is sometimes found a detached and a solitary being," where "he deals with his fellow creatures as he does with his cattle and soil, for the sake of the profits they bring," and where "the bands of affection are broken."[2]

At the same time—and this is particularly interesting for the development of our argument—Ferguson was more willing than Adam Smith to speculate on the wider political consequences of economic expansion. He does so toward the end of the *Essay*, where he starts out in a deceptively orthodox manner:

> It has been found, that, except in a few singular cases, the commercial and political arts have advanced together.

He goes on, still very much along the lines of Montesquieu and Sir James Steuart:

> In some nations the spirit of commerce, intent on securing its profits, has led the way to political wisdom.[3]

He also mentions an argument that was to receive considerable emphasis in later debates, namely, that wealthy citizens might be "formidable to those who pretend to dominion."

But immediately thereafter he dwells, at much greater length, on the reasons for which the preoccupation with individual wealth can lead in the opposite direction, to "despotical government." Among these reasons there are those that had long been standard items in the "republican tradition": the corruption of republics through luxury and prodigality.[4] But Ferguson weaves some remarkably new ideas into that tradition. For example, among the reasons for which "the foundation on which freedom was built, may serve to support a tyranny" he lists the *fear of losing wealth* and situations in which "heirs of family find themselves straitened and poor, in the midst of affluence." Relative deprivation and *ressentiment* resulting from actual or feared downward mobility are here seen as intimately bound up with the acquisitive society and its tumultuous ways, and these feelings are viewed as breeding ground for the ready acceptance of whatever "strong" government promises to stave off such real or imagined dangers.[5] Moreover, commerce creates a desire for tranquility and efficiency, and this may be another source of despotism:

> When we suppose government to have bestowed a degree of tranquillity, which we sometimes hope to reap from it, as the best of its fruits, and public affairs to proceed, in the several departments of legislation and execution, *with the least possible interruption to commerce and lucrative arts*; such a state . . . is more akin to despotism than we are apt to imagine. . . .
> Liberty is never in greater danger than it is when we measure national felicity . . . by the mere tranquillity which may attend on equitable administration.[6]

Here is the other side of Sir James Steuart's metaphor of the economy as a delicate watch. The need to keep it working—to insure tranquility, regularity, and efficiency—is not just a bar to princely caprice. Ferguson perceives correctly that it can be invoked as a key argument for authoritarian rule, as indeed had already been done by the Physiocrats and as was going to happen over and over again during the next two centuries.

Writing under the July Monarchy, almost seventy years after Ferguson, Tocqueville was to express very similar ambivalent feelings about the meaning of economic progress for freedom. In a chapter of *Democracy in America* (1835) he too repeats at first the conventional wisdom:

> I do not know if one can cite a single manufacturing and commercial nation from the Tyrians to the Florentines and the English, that has not also been free. Therefore a close tie and a necessary relation exist between these two things: freedom and industry.[7]

But although this pronouncement has often been quoted,[8] Tocqueville, like Ferguson before him, devotes far more space, in the rest of the chapter, to situations in which the opposite relation prevails. His concern is motivated by the state of France under Louis-Philippe where Guizot had proclaimed *"Enrichissez-vous!"* as a model of conduct for the citizen and where Balzac had written:

> It is a mistake . . . to believe that it is King Louis-Philippe who reigns and he is not deceived on this point. He knows, as well as we do, that above the Constitution is the holy, venerable, solid, amiable,

gracious, beautiful, noble, young, all-powerful five-franc piece!"[9]

This outburst is in effect a paraphrase of those constraints on the prince that Montesquieu and Sir James Steuart discerned and found so hopeful; the passage even recalls Rohan's dictum *l'intérêt commande au prince* once the meaning Rohan gave to *intérêt* is suitably altered in line with its subsequent semantic drift. But neither Balzac nor Tocqueville was prepared to celebrate such a state of affairs.

In focusing on the dangers that material progress can hold for liberty, Tocqueville takes as his point of departure a situation in which "the taste for material enjoyments . . . develops more rapidly than the enlightenments and habits of liberty." Under those conditions, with men neglecting public affairs for the sake of making private fortunes, Tocqueville questions the then already firmly established doctrine of the harmony of private and public interests:

> *These people think they follow the doctrine of interest,* but they have only a crude idea of what it is, and, to watch the better over what they call their business *(leurs affaires),* they neglect the principal part of it which is to remain their own masters.

Here the interests are far from taming or chaining the passions of the rulers; on the contrary, if the citizens become absorbed by the pursuit of their private interests, it will be possible for a "clever and ambitious man to seize power." And Tocqueville directs some superbly caustic and prophetic words (written years before the rise of Napoleon III) at those who, for the sake of a favorable business climate, ask only for "law and order":

A nation that demands from its government nothing but the maintenance of order is already a slave in the bottom of its heart; it is the slave of its wellbeing, and the man who is to chain it can arrive on the scene.[10]

According to Ferguson and Tocqueville, then, economic expansion and the preoccupation with individual economic improvement that goes with it both cause the advance of the political arts and can also be responsible for their deterioration. This thought was later taken up by Marx in his class analysis of the 1848 revolutions: from progressive, the political role of the bourgeoisie turned reactionary as these events unfolded. But the earlier formulations are, in a sense, richer, for they demonstrate that economic expansion is *basically and simultaneously* ambivalent in its political effects, whereas Marxist thought imposes a temporal sequence with the positive effects necessarily antedating the negative ones.

The uneasiness of Ferguson and Tocqueville over the Montesquieu-Steuart doctrine can be summarized in two points. First of all, so they showed, there is another side to the insight that the modern economy, its complex interdependence and growth constitute so delicate a mechanism that the *grands coups d'autorité* of despotic government become impossible. If it is true *that the economy must be deferred to,* then there is a case not only for constraining the imprudent actions of the prince but for repressing those of the people, for limiting participation, in short, for crushing anything that could be interpreted by some economist-king as a threat to the proper functioning of the "delicate watch."

Secondly, Ferguson and Tocqueville implicitly criticized the older tradition of thought that had seen in the pursuit of material interest a welcome alternative to the passionate scramble for glory and power. While not invoking the fallacy of composition, they put forward a rather similar point: as long as *not everyone* is playing the "innocent" game of making money, the total absorption in it of *most* citizens leaves the few who play for the higher stakes of power freer than before to pursue their ambition. In this way social arrangements that substitute the interests for the passions as the guiding principle of human action for the many can have the side effect of killing the civic spirit and of thereby opening the door to tyranny.

In pointing out that the loss of wealth and the fear of such loss may predispose people in favor of tyranny, Ferguson came close to making a final and particularly damaging critique of the general psychological premise on which the optimistic vision of Montesquieu and others had been built—of the thought, that is, that man by pursuing his material interests will become inured against the passions. This idea that had seemed so obvious to those who observed money-making activities from a distance and with some disdain was coupled, as we have seen, with the equally comforting thought that the "lower orders," or the "great mob of mankind," have only interests to pursue and have little time or taste for the passions.

As Hobbes had put it, "All men naturally strive for honour and preferment; but chiefly they who are least troubled with caring for necessary things."[11] And yet this very thought could have led one to expect things to change markedly once economic growth would take hold. To Hobbes the pursuit of the passions was highly income-elastic, as economists would say, and therefore ordinary men could be expected to engage more extensively in passionate behavior as they moved up the income scale. In this manner economic expansion, hailed originally because it would divert man from "striving for honour and preferment," would in the end generate more rather than less passionate behavior, according to the very logic of Hobbes's proposition. Rousseau understood this dynamic well when he wrote:

> . . . With man in society, things are very different: first the necessary must be taken care of, then the superfluous: then come the delights, then the accumulation of immense riches, then of subjects, then of slaves; never is there a moment of respite. What is most remarkable is that the less the needs are natural and pressing the more the passions increase and, what is worse, the power to satisfy them.[12]

But the idea that men pursuing their interests would be forever harmless was decisively given up only when the reality of capitalist development was in full view. As economic growth in the nineteenth and twentieth centuries uprooted millions of people, impoverished numerous groups while enriching some, caused large-scale unemployment during cyclical depressions, and produced modern mass society, it became clear to a number of observers that those caught in these violent transformations would on occasion become passionate—passionately angry, fearful, resentful. There is no need to list here the names of those social scientists who recorded these developments and analyzed them under the terms of alienation, *anomie, ressentiment, Vermassung,* class struggle, and many others. It is precisely because we are under the influence of those analyses, and even more under the impact of cataclysmic events which we try to understand with their help, that the doctrine reviewed here has an air of unreality about it and, on superficial acquaintance, appears not to deserve to be taken seriously.

In the concluding sections of this essay I shall show why, nevertheless, the doctrine was worth reconstructing. As a brief aside it is well to note at this point that the political arguments for capitalism whose career has been outlined here are not the only ones to have been put forward. A currently much more familiar argument states that the existence of private property, and in particular of private property in the means of production, is essential to provide people with a material basis for dissent from and opposition to the authorities of the day. For example, so it is alleged, the right to free speech may be empty if the person who wishes to exercise it has to rely for his very livelihood on the authorities he might wish to criticize. This is not the place either to evaluate that argument or to trace it in any detail; but there can be no doubt that it sounds more plausible to our ears than the one with which we have become acquainted in this essay.

The main support for the "modern" argument comes from the comparison between capitalist and socialist countries with respect to the opportunities for dissent.[b] Little wonder, then, that the argument was not articulated at the time of Montesquieu. Yet its appearance did not wait for the communist regimes of the twentieth century. It was formulated as soon as the institution of private property came under sustained attack and as other conceivable social arrangements were explored in some detail. Thus the modern political argument for

[b] Another reason for the greater plausibility of the argument is that it is slightly more modest: it looks upon capitalism as a necessary condition for political freedom, but not as a sufficient one. See Milton Friedman, *Capitalism and Freedom* (Chicago: University of Chicago Press, 1962), p. 10.

capitalism that is today associated with such authors as Mises, Hayek, and Milton Friedman was originally put forward by none other than Proudhon. Though an eloquent critic of the institution of private property— he is, after all, best known for the dictum "Property is theft"—Proudhon was also fearful of the enormous power of the state. And in his later writings he conceived of the idea of opposing to this power a similar "absolutist" power—that of private property.[13] By the middle of the nineteenth century the experience with capitalism had been such that the argument about the benign effects of *le doux commerce* on human nature had totally changed: it was just because property was now seen as a wild, boundless, and revolutionary force that Proudhon gave it the role of countervailing the equally terrifying power of the state. He actually uses the term "counter-weight" and thereby connects his thesis with the intellectual tradition that has been traced here, just as Galbraith was to do for yet another purpose after one more century.[14] But the substance of Proudhon's thought about the character of property and money-making was at an enormous distance from those who had written about these matters in the preceding century.

The Promise of an Interest-Governed World versus the Protestant Ethic

IN COMPARISON to what ought to be called the Proudhon argument on the political merits of capitalism, the Montesquieu-Steuart doctrine seems odd, if not extravagant. But therein lies much of its interest and value. It is precisely because it strikes the contemporary mind as odd that it can throw some light on the still puzzling ideological circumstances of the rise of capitalism.

An obvious way of entering into this topic is to compare the account of the emergence of money-making as an honored occupation that has been presented in this essay with Weber's thesis on the Protestant ethic and with the debate around it. As was noted repeatedly in the previous pages, the expansion of commerce and industry in the seventeenth and eighteenth centuries has been viewed here as being welcomed and promoted not by some marginal social groups, nor by an insurgent ideology, but by a current of opinion that arose right in the center of the "power structure" and the "establishment" of the time, out of the problems with which the prince and particularly his advisors and other concerned notables were grappling. Ever since the end of the Middle Ages, and particularly as a result of the increasing frequency of war and civil war in the seventeenth and eighteenth centuries, the search was on for a behavioral equivalent for religious precept, for new rules of conduct and devices that would impose much needed discipline and constraints on both rulers and ruled, and the expansion of commerce and industry was thought to hold much promise in this regard.

Weber and his followers as well as most of his critics were primarily interested in the psychological processes through which some groups of men became single-minded in the rational pursuit of capitalist accumulation. My story takes it for granted that some men became so impelled and focuses instead on the reaction to the new phenomenon by what is called today the intellectual, managerial, and administrative elite. That reaction was favorable, not because the money-making activities were approved in themselves, but because they were thought to have a most beneficial side effect: they kept the men who were engaged in them "out of mischief," as it were, and had, more specifically, the virtue of imposing restraints on princely caprice, arbitrary government, and adventurous foreign policies. Weber claims that capitalistic behavior and activities were the indirect (and originally unintended) result of a desperate *search for individual salvation*. My claim is that the diffusion of capitalist forms owed much to an equally desperate search for a way of *avoiding society's ruin*, permanently threatening at the time because of precarious arrangements for internal and external order. Clearly both claims could be valid at the same time: one relates to the motivations of the aspiring new elites, the other to those of various gatekeepers. But Weber's thesis has attracted so much attention that the latter topic has been totally overlooked.

A further important difference exists between Weber's thesis and the current of ideas that has been retraced here. Weber suggested that Calvin's doctrine of predestination resulted, among his followers, not in fatalism, nor in a frantic search for earthly pleasures, but—curiously and counterintuitively—in methodical activity informed by purpose and self-denial. This thesis was more than a magnificent paradox; it spelled out one of those remarkable unintended effects of human actions (or, in this case, thoughts) whose discovery has become the peculiar province and highest ambition of the social scientist since Vico, Mandeville, and Adam Smith. Now I submit—on the basis of the story I have told here—that discoveries of the symmetrically opposite kind are both possible and valuable. On the one hand, there is no doubt that human actions and social decisions tend to have consequences that were entirely unintended at the outset. But, on the other hand, these actions and decisions are often taken because they are *earnestly and fully expected to have certain effects that then wholly fail to materialize.* The latter phenomenon, while being the structural obverse of the former, is also likely to be one of its causes; the illusory expectations that are associated with certain social decisions at the time of their adoption help keep their *real* future effects from view.

Here lies one of the principal reasons for which the phenomenon is of interest: the expectation of large, if unrealistic, benefits obviously serves to facilitate certain social decisions. Exploration and discovery of such expectations therefore help render social change more intelligible.

Curiously, the intended but unrealized effects of social decisions stand in need of being discovered even more than those effects that were unintended but turn out to be all too real: the latter are at least *there,* whereas the intended but unrealized effects are only to be found in the expressed expectations of social actors at a certain, often fleeting, moment of time. Moreover, once these desired effects fail to happen and refuse to come into the world, the fact that they were originally counted on is likely to be not only forgotten but actively repressed. This is not just a matter of the original actors keeping their self-respect, but is essential if the succeeding power holders are to be assured of the legitimacy of the new order: what social order could long survive the dual awareness that it was adopted with the firm expectation that it would solve certain problems, and that it clearly and abysmally fails to do so?

Contemporary Notes

THE extent to which the ideas that have been discussed in this essay have been erased from the collective consciousness can be gauged by recalling some contemporary critiques of capitalism. In one of the most attractive and influential of these critiques, the stress is on the repressive and alienating feature of capitalism, on the way it inhibits the development of the "full human personality." From the vantage point of the present essay, this accusation seems a bit unfair, for capitalism was precisely expected and supposed to repress certain human drives and proclivities and to fashion a less multifaceted, less unpredictable, and more "one-dimensional" human personality. This position, which seems so strange today, arose from extreme anguish over the clear and present dangers of a certain historical period, from concern over the destructive forces unleashed by the human passions with the only exception, so it seemed at the time, of "innocuous" avarice. *In sum, capitalism was supposed to accomplish exactly what was soon to be denounced as its worst feature.*

For as soon as capitalism was triumphant and "passion" seemed indeed to be restrained and perhaps even extinguished in the comparatively peaceful, tranquil, and business-minded Europe of the period after the Congress of Vienna, the world suddenly appeared empty, petty, and boring and the stage was set for the Romantic critique of the bourgeois order as incredibly impoverished in relation to earlier ages—the new world seemed to lack nobility, grandeur, mystery, and, above all, passion. Considerable traces of this nostalgic critique can be found in subsequent social thought from Fourier's advocacy of passionate attraction to Marx's theory of alienation, and from Freud's thesis of libidinal repression as the price of progress to Weber's concept of *Entzauberung* (progressive disintegration of the magical vision of the world). In all of these explicit or implicit critiques of capitalism there was little recognition that, to an earlier age, the world of the "full human personality," replete with diverse passions, appeared as a menace that needed to be exorcized to the greatest possible extent.

The opposite kind of forgetfulness is also in evidence: it consists of trotting out the identical ideas that had been put forward at an earlier period, without any references to the encounter they had already had with reality, an encounter that is seldom wholly satisfactory. To open a brief parenthesis, it may be remarked that Santayana's maxim "those who do not remember the past are condemned to repeat it" is more likely to hold rigorously for the history of *ideas* than for the history of events. The latter, as we all know, never quite repeats itself; but *vaguely similar* circumstances at two different and perhaps distant points of time may very well give rise to *identical and identically flawed* thought-responses if the earlier intellectual episode has been forgotten. The reason is of course that thought abstracts from a number of circumstances which it holds to be nonessential but which constitute the uniqueness of every single historical situation.

This literal and deplorable correctness of Santayana's maxim as applied to the history of ideas can be illustrated here at the highest level of contemporary social thought. After the story that has been told it is almost painful to see a Keynes resort, in his characteristically low-key defense of capitalism, to the identical argument that was used by Dr. Johnson and other eighteenth-century figures:

> Dangerous human proclivities can be canalized into comparatively harmless channels by the existence of opportunity for money-making and private wealth, which, if they cannot be satisfied in this way, may find their outlet in cruelty, the reckless pursuit of personal power and authority, and other forms of self-aggrandizement. It is better that a man should tyrannize over his bank balance than over his fellow-citizens; and whilst the former is sometimes denounced as being but a means to the latter, sometimes at least it is an alternative.[c]

Here is the old idea of money-making as an "innocent" pastime and outlet for men's energies, as an institution that diverts men from the antagonistic competition for power to the somewhat ridiculous and distasteful, but essentially harmless accumulation of wealth.

Another important figure who made a strong, if indirect, case for capitalism on the basis of its beneficial political consequences was Schumpeter. In his theory of imperialism[15] Schumpeter argued that territorial ambition, the desire for colonial expansion, and the warlike spirit in general were not the inevitable consequence of the capitalist system, as the Marxists would have it.

---

[c] *The General Theory of Employment Interest and Money* (London: Macmillan, 1936), p. 374. In what amounts to a caricature of this view, Hayek has argued in defense of the institution of inheritance on the ground that bequeathing wealth is a socially less harmful way of bestowing unearned benefits on one's children than actively seeking preferred positions for them during one's lifetime. That the one does by no means exclude the other is particularly obvious in this case. See F. A. Hayek, *The Constitution of Liberty* (Chicago: University of Chicago Press, 1960), p. 91.

Rather, they resulted from residual, precapitalist mentalities that unfortunately were strongly embedded among the ruling groups of the major European powers. For Schumpeter, capitalism itself could not possibly make for conquest and war: its spirit was rational, calculating, and therefore averse to risk-taking on the scale implicit in warmaking and in other heroic antics. Interesting as they were as a counterpoint to the various Marxist theories of imperialism, Schumpeter's views evinced less awareness of the knottiness of the problem he was dealing with than those of Adam Ferguson and Tocqueville that have just been recalled. To go back even further: Cardinal de Retz, with his insistence that the passions are not to be counted out in situations where interest-motivated behavior is considered to be the rule, appears to have had the better part of the argument than either Keynes or Schumpeter.

I conclude that both critics and defenders of capitalism could improve upon their arguments through knowledge of the episode in intellectual history that has been recounted here. This is probably all one can ask of history, and of the history of ideas in particular: not to resolve issues, but to raise the level of the debate.

NOTES

1. *The Protestant Ethic and the Spirit of Capitalism*, tr. Talcott Parsons (New York: Scribner's, 1958), p. 74.

2. See Werner Sombart, *Der Bourgeois* (Munich: Duncker and Humblot, 1913); Joseph A. Schumpeter, *History of Economic Analysis* (New York: Oxford University Press, 1954), p. 91; and Raymond de Roover, "The Scholastic Attitude Toward Trade and Entrepreneurship," now reprinted in de Roover, *Business, Banking and Economic Thought*, ed. Julius Kirshner (Chicago: University of Chicago Press, 1974); see also the introductory essay by Kirshner, pp. 16–18.

3. See Herbert A. Deane, *The Political and Social Ideas of St. Augustine* (New York: Columbia University Press, 1963), pp. 44–56.

4. *Ibid.*, pp. 52 and 268.

5. *Esprit des lois*, Book III, Chapter 7. All translations are mine unless noted otherwise.

6. The conflict of these two intellectual traditions is documented in María Rosa Lida de Malkiel, *La idea de la fama en la Edad Media Castellana* (Mexico: Fondo de Cultura Económica, 1952). See also the French translation of this work, which bears the more appropriate title *L'idée de la gloire dans la tradition occidentale* (Paris: Klincksieck, 1968).

7. *Ibid.*, Chapters 1 and 2. The continuity of the medieval chivalric ethos with the aristocratic ideal of the Renaissance is also stressed by Paul Bénichou, *Morales du grand siècle* (Paris: Gallimard, Collection Idées, 1948), pp. 20–23 and, in a polemic with Burckhardt, by Johan Huizinga, *The Waning of the Middle Ages* (New York: Doubleday, 1945), pp. 40 and 69ff.

8. Bénichou, *ibid.*, pp. 15–79. For the thesis that Corneille's heroes and their projects all end up as failures, see Serge Doubrovsky, *Corneille et la dialectique du héros* (Paris: Gallimard, 1963).

9. This is Bénichou's forceful phrase in *Morales*, pp. 155–180.

10. See the convincing demonstration, in a polemic with C. B. Macpherson, of Keith Thomas in "Social Origins of Hobbes's

Political Thought" in K. C. Brown, ed., *Hobbes Studies* (Oxford: Blackwell, 1965).

11. Bénichou, *Morales*, pp. 262–267, 285–299.

12. *The Prince*, Chapter XV.

13. See the Introduction by Richard S. Peters to *Body, Man, Citizen: Selections from Thomas Hobbes*, ed. Peters (New York: Collier, 1962).

14. Part III, Introduction.

15. Pars. 131–132, in Giambattista Vico, *Opere*, ed. Fausto Nicolini (Milan: Ricciardi, 1953).

16. See Deane, *Political and Social Ideas of St. Augustine*, Chapter IV, and Michael Walzer's account of Calvin's political thought under the title "The State as an Order of Repression" in *The Revolution of the Saints* (Cambridge, Mass.: Harvard University Press), pp. 30–48.

17. *Scienza nuova*, pars. 132–133; see also 130 and 135.

18. *Works*, ed. J. Spedding et al. (London, 1859), Vol. III, p. 418.

19. *Ibid.*, p. 438. My emphasis.

20. Leo Strauss, *The Political Philosophy of Hobbes* (Oxford: Clarendon Press, 1936), p. 92; and Rachael M. Kydd, *Reason and Conduct in Hume's Treatise* (New York: Russell & Russell, 1946), p. 116.

21. Part IV, Prop. 7. Translation by W. H. White revised by A. H. Stirling (London: Oxford University Press, 1927).

22. Part IV, Prop. 14.

23. Part V, Prop. 42.

24. Kydd, *Hume's Treatise*, pp. viii, 38, 156–162.

25. *Treatise*, Book II, Part III, Section III.

26. *Ibid.*, Book III, Part II, Section II.

27. "Of Refinement in the Arts" in David Hume, *Writings on Economics*, ed. E. Rotwein (Madison, Wis.: University of Wisconsin Press, 1970), pp. 31–32.

28. *Essays Moral, Political, and Literary*, ed. T. H. Green and T. H. Grose (London: Longmans, 1898), Vol. I, pp. 226–227.

29. Franco Venturi, *Utopia e riforma nell'Illuminismo* (Torino: Einaudi, 1970), p. 99. Here Venturi sketches the remarkable career of the author of this article, Alexandre Deleyre.

30. *Oeuvres complètes* (Paris: Hachette, 1968), Vol. I, p. 239.

31. *Système de la nature* (Hildesheim: Georg Olms, 1966, reproduction of 1821 Paris edition), pp. 424–425.

32. D. W. Smith, *Helvétius*, pp. 133–135.

33. *De l'esprit* (Paris, 1758), pp. 159–160. My emphasis.

34. On this topic, see Arthur O. Lovejoy, *Reflections on Human Nature* (The Johns Hopkins Press, 1961), Lecture II: "The Theory of Human Nature in the American Constitution and the Method of Counterpoise"; Richard Hofstadter, *The American Political Tradition and the Men Who Made It* (New York: Alfred A. Knopf, 1948), Chapter I: "The Founding Fathers: An Age of Realism"; and Martin Diamond, "The American Idea of Man: The View from the Founding" in Irving Kristol and Paul Weaver, eds., *The Americans 1976* (Lexington, Mass.: D. C. Heath, 1976), Vol. II, pp. 1–23.

35. *Leviathan*, Chapter 13.

36. Friedrich Meinecke, *Die Idee der Staatsräson in der neueren Geschichte* (Munich: R. Oldenbourg, 1924), pp. 85ff.

37. *Ibid.*, p. 184.

38. *Ibid.*, pp. 52–55.

39. *Ibid.*, p. 211.

40. *Analogy of Religion* in *Works* (Oxford: Clarendon Press, 1896), Vol. I, pp. 97–98.

41. *Characteristicks of Men, Manners, Opinions, Times*, reprint of the 1711 edn. (Indianapolis: Bobbs-Merrill, 1964), pp. 332 and 336 (italics in the text).

42. *Treatise*, Book III, Part II, Section II.

43. La Rochefoucauld, *Oeuvres* (Paris: Hachette, 1923), Vol. I, p. 30.

44. Jean de Silhon, *De la certitude des connaissances humaines* (Paris, 1661), pp. 104–105.

45. *Wealth of Nations*, ed. E. Cannan (New York: Modern Library, 1937), p. 325.

46. Letter of April 9, 1513, in *Opere* (Milan: Ricciardi, 1963), p. 1100.

47. A survey of the French seventeenth-century literature is in F. E. Sutcliffe, *Guez de Balzac et son temps—littérature et politique* (Paris: Nizet, 1959), pp. 120–131. On the changing ranking of avarice among the deadly sins in the Middle Ages, see Morton Bloomfield, *The Seven Deadly Sins* (East Lansing, Mich.: Michigan State College Press, 1954), p. 95.

48. Gunn, "Interest," p. 559, note 37.

49. *De l'esprit*, p. 53.

50. *Politique tirée des propres paroles de l'Ecriture Sainte*, ed. J. LeBrun (Geneva: Droz, 1962), p. 24, and A. J. Krailsheimer, *Studies in Self-Interest from Descartes to La Bruyère* (Oxford: Clarendon Press, 1962), p. 184.

51. *Tractatus theologico-politicus*, Chapter V, in Spinoza, *The Political Works*, ed. A. G. Wernham (Oxford: Clarendon Press, 1958), p. 93.

52. The Marquis of Halifax as quoted in Raab, *The English Face of Machiavelli*, p. 247.

53. *Les caractères* (Paris: Garnier, 1932), p. 133.

54. Shaftesbury, *Characteristicks*, p. 76, quoted in Jacob Viner, *The Role of Providence in the Social Order* (Philadelphia: American Philosophical Society, 1972), p. 70.

55. *Analogy*, p. 121, note.

56. Cited from a 1649 catechism in R. Koebner, "Despot and Despotism: Vicissitudes of a Political Term," *Journal of the Warburg and Courtauld Institutes* 14 (1951), p. 293.

57. *History of England* (London, 1782), VI, p. 127; cited in Giuseppe Giarrizzo, *David Hume politico e storico* (Turin: Einaudi, 1962), p. 209.

58. Felix Gilbert, *Machiavelli and Guicciardini* (Princeton, N. J.: Princeton University Press, 1965), p. 157.

59. Gunn, "Interest," p. 557.

60. Gunn, *Politics*, p. 160.

61. *Inquiry into the Principles of Political Oeconomy* (1767), ed. A. S. Skinner (Chicago: University of Chicago Press, 1966), Vol. I, pp. 143–144.

62. Charles Herle, *Wisdomes Tripos . . .* (London, 1655), cited in Gunn, "Interest," p. 557.

63. *Characters and Passages from Notebooks*, ed. A. R. Waller (Cambridge: University Press, 1908), p. 394; see also Gunn, "Interest," pp. 558–559.

64. Gunn, *Politics*, Ch. IV.

65. *Ethics*, Part IV, Prop. 33.

66. See Leonard Krieger, *The Politics of Discretion: Pufendorf and the Acceptance of Natural Law* (Chicago: Chicago University Press, 1965), p. 119.

67. Peter Laslett, "Introduction," in John Locke, *Two Treatises of Government*, ed. Laslett (Cambridge: University Press, 2nd edn. 1967), p. 74.

68. *Two Treatises,* II, par. 127.

69. *Ibid.,* par. 22.

70. *Essays,* Vol. I, p. 160.

71. Chapter 39.

72. *Esprit des lois,* XX, 4.

73. *Philosophie des Geldes* (Leipzig: Duncker and Humblot, 1900), p. 232.

74. *Boswell's Life of Johnson* (New York: Oxford University Press, 1933), Vol. I, p. 567. The date is March 27, 1775.

75. *Réflexions et maximes* in *Oeuvres* (Paris: Cité des livres, 1929), Vol. II, p. 151.

76. Salvador de Madariaga, *The Fall of the Spanish-American Empire* (London: Hollis and Carter, 1947), p. 7. My emphasis.

77. Quoted in François de Forbonnais, *Recherches et considérations sur les finances de France, depuis l'année 1595 jusqu'à l'année 1721* (Basle, 1758), Vol. I, p. 436.

78. Jacques Savary, *Le parfait négociant, ou Instruction générale de tout ce qui regarde le commerce* (Paris, 1675), 1713 edn., p. 1 (italics in the original).

79. Viner, *Providence,* pp. 36ff.

80. *Esprit des lois,* XX, 1.

81. *Règlement intérieur du Collège Louis-le-Grand* (1769), p. 36. This document was Exhibit No. 163 in the Exhibition of Daily Life in Paris in the Eighteenth Century, Archives Nationales, Paris, summer 1974.

82. *Characteristicks,* p. 336.

83. *A System of Moral Philosophy,* facsimile of 1755 edn. in *Works* (Hildesheim: Georg Olms, 1969), Vol. V, p. 12.

84. *Treatise,* Book II, Part III, Section IV.

85. *Wealth of Nations,* p. 324. My emphasis.

86. *Writings on Economics,* p. 53.

PART TWO

1. V, 6.

2. XXI, 20.

3. XXII, 13.

4. XX, 23.

5. Chapter VI, par. 12; see Spinoza, *The Political Works,* p. 321.

6. Chapter VII, par. 8; *ibid.,* pp. 341–343.

7. Cf. Alexandre Matheron, *Individu et communauté chez Spinoza* (Paris: Minuit, 1969), pp. 176–178.

8. *Oeuvres complètes* (Paris: Pléiade, NRF, 1949), Vol. I, p. 112.

9. *Esprit des lois*, XI, 4.

10. *Ibid.*

11. Introduction in Coleman, ed., *Revisions in Mercantilism*, pp. 15–16.

12. *Essai politique sur le commerce* (1734) in E. Daire, *Economistes français du 17ᶜ siècle* (Paris, 1843), p. 733.

13. XX, 2.

14. *Ibid.*

15. *Essai politique*, p. 733. An extended argument that there is a great deal of glory in commerce is made in Abbé Gabriel François Coyer, *La noblesse commerçante* (London, 1756), and in Louis de Sacy, *Traité de la gloire* (Paris, 1715), pp. 99–100.

16. See Ronald L. Meek, *Economics and Ideology and Other Essays* (London: Chapman and Hall, 1967), particularly his 1954 essay "The Scottish Contribution to Marxist Sociology," pp. 34–50.

17. *Inquiry*, Vol. I, p. 181 (italics mine).

18. *Ibid.*, p. 213.

19. See Paul Chamley, *Economie politique et philosophie chez Steuart et Hegel* (Paris: Dalloz, 1963), and *Documents relatifs à Sir James Steuart* (Paris: Dalloz, 1965), pp. 89–92 and 143–147.

20. *Inquiry*, Vol. I, pp. 215–217.

21. *Ibid.*, pp. 278–279.

22. See Chapter 9, "Steuart's Economics of Control," in S. R. Sen, *The Economics of Sir James Steuart* (London: B. Bell and Sons, 1957), and R. L. Meek, "The Economics of Control Prefigured," *Science and Society*, Fall 1958.

23. *Inquiry*, Vol. I, p. 278.

24. *Ibid.*, p. 217.

25. Popularized by Leibniz and Voltaire, its use is traced to Nicolas Oresmus (died A.D. 1382) in Lynn White, *Medieval Technology and Social Change* (Oxford: Clarendon Press, 1963), p. 125; see also Carlo M. Cipolla, *Clocks and Culture, 1300–1700* (London: Collins, 1967), pp. 105, 165.

26. William C. Lehmann, *John Millar of Glasgow, 1735–1801* (Cambridge: University Press, 1960), pp. 330–331. The major works of Millar are reprinted in Parts III and IV of this book.

NOTES

27. *Ibid.*, p. 336.
28. *Ibid.*, pp. 337–339 (italics mine).
29. Cited in E. P. Thompson, *The Making of the English Working Class* (New York: Vintage Books, 1963), p. 361.
30. Since Millar's essay was found after his death in 1801, it is difficult to date it.
31. George Rudé, *Wilkes and Liberty: A Social Study of 1763 to 1774* (Oxford: Clarendon Press, 1962), pp. 179–184. See also Frank Ackerman, "Riots, Populism, and Non-Industrial Labor: A Comparative Study of the Political Economy of the Urban Crowd" (unpublished Ph.D. thesis, Harvard University, Department of Economics, 1974), Chapter 2.
32. The suppressed passage is reproduced as a footnote in *Essays*, Vol. I, p. 97. The episode is discussed in Giarrizzo, *David Hume*, p. 82.
33. Pauline Maier, "Popular Uprisings and Civil Authority in Eighteenth-Century America," *William and Mary Quarterly* 27 (Jan. 1970), p. 18; see also Dirk Hoerder, "People and Mobs: Crowd Action in Massachusetts during the American Revolution" (unpublished dissertation, Freie Universität, Berlin, 1971), pp. 129–137.
34. Maier, *ibid.*, p. 27.
35. See Ronald L. Meek, *The Economics of Physiocracy* (Cambridge, Mass.: Harvard University Press, 1963).
36. See A. S. Skinner's Introduction to Steuart's *Inquiry*, Vol. I, p. xxxvii, and Chamley, *Documents*, pp. 71–74.
37. *Wealth of Nations*, pp. 800, 880.
38. From the "Extract from 'Rural Philosophy'" included in Meek, *Physiocracy*, p. 63.
39. Jacob Viner, "Adam Smith and Laissez Faire," *Journal of Political Economy* 35 (April 1927), pp. 198–232.
40. Article "Hommes" (1757) in *François Quesnay et la Physiocratie* (I.N.E.D., 1958), Vol. II, p. 570.
41. *Leviathan*, Chapter 19.
42. The terminology is due to Le Mercier de la Rivière.
43. On this aspect of Physiocratic thought, see Mario Einaudi, *The Physiocratic Doctrine of Judicial Control* (Cambridge, Mass.: Harvard University Press, 1938).

NOTES

44. Ed. E. Depître (Paris, 1910), Chapters 19 and 44; see also Georges Weulersse, *Le mouvement physiocratique en France, 1756–1770* (Paris: Alcan, 1910), Vol. II, pp. 44–61.
45. *Théories des lois civiles* (London, 1774), Vol. I, pp. 118–119 (*Oeuvres*, III).
46. Their considerable influence on public policy and on the climate of opinion is traced in Weulersse, *Le mouvement physiocratique*, Vol. II, Book 4.
47. Modern Library edn., p. 385.
48. *Ibid.*, p. 388.
49. *Ibid.*, p. 389.
50. *Ibid.*, p. 391.
51. *Ibid.*, p. 390.
52. David Hume, *The History of England* (Oxford, 1826), Vol. V, p. 430 (Appendix III "Manners"), and Adam Smith, *Lectures on Justice, Police, Revenue and Arms*, ed. E. Cannan (Oxford: Clarendon Press, 1896), pp. 42–43.
53. *Wealth of Nations*, p. 460.
54. *Ibid.*, p. 638.
55. *Ibid.*, p. 508.
56. Some recent commentaries are in Nathan Rosenberg, "Adam Smith on the Division of Labor: Two Views or One?" *Economica* 32 (May 1965), pp. 127–139, and Robert L. Heilbroner, "The Paradox of Progress: Decline and Decay in *The Wealth of Nations*," *Journal of the History of Ideas* 34 (April-June 1973), pp. 242–262.
57. *Wealth of Nations*, p. 735.
58. *Lectures*, p. 257.
59. *Ibid.*, p. 259.
60. *Ibid.*, pp. 253–255.
61. For a full history and analysis of this republican current of political thought from Machiavelli to the eighteenth century in England and America, see Pocock, *Machiavellian Moment*.
62. *Wealth of Nations*, p. 324.
63. *The Theory of Moral Sentiments*, 9th edn. (London, 1801), Vol. I, pp. 98–99 (italics mine). This and a number of similar and complementary passages are cited in an interesting article by Nathan Rosenberg, "Adam Smith, Consumer Tastes, and Economic Growth," *Journal of Political Economy* 7 (May-June

1968), pp. 361–374. As Lovejoy has pointed out, this train of thought is a striking anticipation of the idea of "conspicuous consumption," which is one of the mainstays of Veblen's *Theory of the Leisure Class*. See Lovejoy, *Reflections*, pp. 208–215.

64. See *Emile*, Part IV, and *Discours sur l'origine et les fondements de l'inégalité parmi les hommes*, note o.

65. Cited in Lovejoy, *Reflections*, p. 146.

66. *Wealth of Nations*, pp. 594–595 (italics mine).

67. *Discourses*, Book I, Chapter LXVIII.

68. *English Works*, Vol. II, p. 160, cited in Keith Thomas, "The Social Origins of Hobbes's Political Thought," in Brown, ed., *Hobbes Studies*, p. 191.

69. See Erich Auerbach, *Mimesis: The Representation of Reality in Western Literature* (Princeton, N. J.: Princeton University Press, 1953), pp. 139–141 and passim.

PART THREE

1. Cited in Emmanuel Chill, ed., *Power, Property and History: Joseph Barnave's Introduction to the French Revolution and Other Writings* (New York: Harper, 1971), p. 142.

2. *Essay on the History of Civil Society*, edited, with an introduction, by Duncan Forbes (Edinburgh: University Press, 1966), p. 19.

3. *Ibid.*, p. 261.

4. See Pocock, *Machiavellian Moment*, for an exhaustive treatment, from Machiavelli to Hamilton.

5. *Essay*, p. 262.

6. *Essay*, pp. 268–269 (emphasis mine).

7. Vol. 2, Part 2, Chapter 14.

8. John U. Nef used it as the epigraph for his well-known two-part essay, "Industrial Europe at the time of the Reformation," *Journal of Political Economy* 49 (Feb.-April 1941), p. 1.

9. Cited (in English) in Harry Levin, *The Gates of Horn* (New York: Oxford University Press, 1963), pp. 152–153, from *La Cousine Bette* (Paris: Conard, 1914), p. 342.

10. Vol. 2, Part 2, Chapter 14.

11. *English Works*, Vol. II, p. 160, cited in Keith Thomas, "The

NOTES

Social Origins of Hobbes's Political Thought," in Brown, ed.,
Hobbes Studies, p. 191.

12. *Discours sur l'origine et les fondements de l'inégalité parmi
les hommes*, note i.

13. This idea is developed at length in Proudhon's posthumous
Théorie de la propriété, in *Oeuvres complètes* (Paris, 1866), Vol.
27, pp. 37, 134–138, 189–212.

14. John Kenneth Galbraith, *American Capitalism: The Concept
of Countervailing Power* (Boston: Houghton Mifflin, 1952).

15. "The Sociology of Imperialisms" (1917), in *Imperialism and
Social Classes* (New York: Kelley, 1951).

INDEX

Ackerman, Frank, 142
alienation, 126, 133
American Constitution, countervailing passion concept in, 28–30
anomie, 126
Aquinas, St. Thomas, 11
arbitrage, foreign exchange, 76, 77, 78, 81–82
aristocratic ideal: honor and glory in, 10–11; and money-making, 58–59, 63; and passions, 112
Auerbach, Erich, 144
Augustine, St., 9–12, 15, 20, 44
authority: abuses of, 96; *grands coups d'autorité*, 72, 74, 76, 78, 81, 86, 88, 96, 124; rebellions against, 89–93; restrictions on, *see* power, restrictions on
avarice: as countervailing passion, 54–55, 108; as sin, 9, 12, 20–21, 41

Bacon, Francis, 21–23, 28
Balzac, Honoré de, 122–23
Barnave, Joseph, 118–19, 144
Bénichou, Paul, 136, 137
Bien, David, viii
bills of exchange, 74n, 81–82; Montesquieu on, 72–74, 76–78
Bloomfield, Morton, 138
Boccalini, Trajano, 34
Bolingbroke, Henry St. John, Viscount, 57, 77
Bonaventura, Federico, 34
Bossuet, Jacques Bénigne, Bishop, 44

Boswell, James, 140
Bourdieu, Pierre, viii
bourgeois ethos and heroic ideal, 12
Brown, K. C., 137, 144, 145
Butler, Joseph, Bishop, 35, 46–47
Butler, Samuel, 50

Calvin, John, 15, 130
capitalism, 9; arguments for, 127–28; and attitudes toward commerce, 59; contemporary ideas on, 132–35; modern, 126–28; Smith's attitude toward, 105, 107; and Weber's Protestant ethic, 129–30
Cervantes Saavedra, Miguel de, 11
Chamley, Paul, 141
Child, Sir Josiah, 79
Chill, Emmanuel, 144
Chinard, Gilbert, 17n
chivalry, ideal of, 10
Cipolla, Carlo M., 141
class struggle, 126
clockmaker, metaphor of, 87
Colbert, Jean Baptiste, 79
commerce: attitudes toward, 51–52; Barnave's ideas on, 118–19; as harmless and *doux*, 58–63, 107, 128; international, 79; Montesquieu's ideas on, 60, 70–80; noncommercial meanings of word, 61–62; Smith's ideas on, 100–102, 104–7; Steuart's ideas on, 81–83
communism, 127

Communist Manifesto, 56
Congress of Vienna, 132
Constitution of United States, countervailing passion concept in, 28–30
Corneille, Pierre, 11, 136
corruption, changing meaning of, 40n
countervailing passions, 20–31, 41, 78
Covenant, Hobbes's concept of, 15, 131–32
Coyer, Gabriel François, 141
Craftsman, The, 57, 77
Cropsey, Joseph, 104n
Cunning of Reason, 17, 19

Daire, E., 141
Dante Alighieri, 11, 20–21
Deane, Herbert A., 136, 137
Deleyre, Alexandre, 137
de Roover, Raymond, 136
despotism: Physiocrats' ideas on, 98, 99; Steuart's ideas on, 85, 99
Diamond, Martin, 138
Domat, Jean, 17n
Doubrovsky, Serge, 136
Durkheim, Emile, 120

economic expansion: Ferguson's view of, 120, 124; Millar's view of, 88–93; Montesquieu-Steuart doctrines examined, 117–18, 120, 123, 124, 128; Montesquieu's view of, 78–80, 87; in nineteenth and twentieth centuries, problems of, 126–27; and passions, Hobbes and Rousseau on, 125–26; Physiocrats' views of, 93–96; Smith's view of, 93–94, 96, 100–12; Steuart's view of, 82–87; and Weber's Protestant ethic, 129–30
Einaudi, Mario, 142–43
elites and capitalism, 129–30
Encyclopédie, 27
Engels, Friedrich, 56, 62n
England: balance of interests in, 51; interest, concept of, 36–37; moral philosophy in, 64; speculation and political corruption in, 57
Enlightenment, 47

fallacy of composition, 119, 125
Federalist, The, 29–30
Ferguson, Adam, 57, 81, 88, 107, 119–22, 124–25, 135
feudalism, Smith on, 100–101
Forbes, Duncan, 104n, 144
Forbonnais, François de, 140
foreign exchange arbitrage, Montesquieu's view of, 76, 77, 78, 81
fortune, changing meaning of, 40n
Fourier, François Marie Charles, 132–33
France: attitude toward commerce, 59–63; heroic ideal demolished in, 11; interest, concept of, 36, 38–39
French Revolution, 113
Freud, Sigmund, 17, 133
Friedman, Milton, 127n, 128

Galbraith, John Kenneth, 128, 145
Galileo Galilei, 13
Giarrizzo, Giuseppe, 139, 142
Gilbert, Felix, 139
glory, pursuit of, 9–12
God as clockmaker, 87

Goethe, Johann Wolfgang von, 19

government: Physiocrats' ideas on, 96–99; restrictions on power, *see* power, restrictions on; Smith's doctrines on, 100–104; tranquility and order in, 121–24

grands coups d'autorité, 72, 74, 76, 78, 81, 86, 88, 96, 124

Guizot, François, 122

Gunn, J. A. W., 36n, 37n, 138, 139

Halifax, George Savile, Marquis of, 45, 46, 139

Hamilton, Alexander, 29, 30, 45n

harmony-of-interests doctrine, 98, 123

Hartz, Louis, 44n

Hayek, F. A., 128, 134n

Hegel, Georg Wilhelm Friedrich, 83; Cunning of Reason, concept, 17, 19

Heilbroner, Robert L., 143

Helvétius, Claude Adrien, 27–28, 43

Herder, Johann Gottfried von, 19

Herle, Charles, 139

heroic ideal, 11–12, 58

Hobbes, Thomas, 11–14, 42, 52, 53, 77, 98, 108–9, 111–12, 125–26; Covenant, concept of, 15, 31–32; on monarchy, 97

Hoerder, Dirk, 142

Hofstadter, Richard, 138

Holbach, Paul Henri Dietrich, Baron d', 27

honor, pursuit of, 11, 108

Huizinga, Johan, 136

human nature, 13, 15, 24, 27, 30, 44n, 49, 66; and capitalism, 132; Hobbes and Rousseau on, 109, 125–26; Smith on, 108–10

Hume, David, 25–26, 37, 47–48, 56, 64, 83, 88, 92, 102, 105n, 137, 143; on love of gain, 54, 54–55n, 65–66; on public debt, 75–76n

Hutcheson, Francis, 64, 65

industry, Smith's ideas on, 100–102

interest: definition of, 32–33; economic, 51–52; as new paradigm, 42–48; and passions, dichotomy of, 42–48, 58, 63–64, 69–70, 73, 102, 125–26; and passions, Smith's attitude toward, 110–11; passions tamed by, 31–42; in politics, 50–51; of prince or state, 33–36; Smith's doctrine of self-interest, 100–12

"Interest Governs the World," 43, 46, 48; predictability and constancy of interest-governed world, 48–56; Protestant ethic and interest-governed world, 128–31

"Interest Will Not Lie," 40, 42–43, 49, 50

interests: balance of, 51; definition of, 32; of groups and individuals, 36–42; harmony-of-interests doctrine, 98, 123; identity of, Hobbes's doctrine, 97–98; passions tamed by, 31–42

international relations: commerce, 79, 81–82; war, 79, 80

Invisible Hand, 105; anticipations of Smith's concept, 10, 16, 17

Johnson, Samuel, 56, 134; on avarice, 55; on money-making, 57–58, 59

Kant, Immanuel, 21
Katzenellenbogen, Adolf, 21n
Keohane, Nannerl O., 17n
Keynes, John Maynard, 86, 133–34, 135
Kirshner, Julius, 136
Koebner, R., 139
Krailsheimer, A. J., 139
Kramnick, Isaac, 57n
Krieger, Leonard, 139

La Bruyère, Jean de, 46, 73n
laissez-faire, 97–98, 104
La Rochefoucauld, François de, 11, 12, 15, 38–39, 42, 138
Laslett, Peter, 139–40
Lehmann, William C., 142
Leibniz, Gottfried Wilhelm von, 141
Le Mercier de la Rivière, Paul Pierre, 98, 142
Levin, Harry, 144
Lévy-Bruhl, Henri, 74n
liberty: Ferguson's ideas on, 121; spirit of, Millar on, 88–90; Tocqueville on, 122
Linguet, Simon Nicolas Henri, 99
Locke, John, 89, 139–40; state of nature, concept, 53–54
Louis XIV, 38
Louis-Philippe, 122–23
Lovejoy, Arthur O., 138, 144
lust, sexual, 9
luxury: and commerce, Smith's view of, 101–2, 106; Mandeville's view of, 18; passion for, 18

Mably, Gabriel Bonnet de, 57
Machiavelli, Niccolò, 13–14, 40n, 49, 53, 111, 137; interest, concept of, 33, 41
machine, metaphor of, 90, 93–94
Macpherson, C. B., 136
Madariaga, Salvador de, 140
Madison, James, 30
Maier, Pauline, 142
Malkiel, Maria Rosa Lida de, 136
Malthus, Thomas R., 86
man as he really is, 12–14, 27–28. See also human nature
Mandeville, Bernard, 18, 19, 25, 112, 119, 130
Marx, Karl, 56, 62, 120, 124
Marxism, 99–100, 134, 135
Matheron, Alexandre, 141
Meek, Ronald L., 141, 142
Meinecke, Friedrich, 33–35, 138
Melon, Jean-François, 80
mercantile class, 91; rise of, 101–2
mercantilism, 52, 79, 82, 83
Middle Ages, pursuit of honor, glory, and riches in, 9–10
middle class, 83; rise of, 101–2
Millar, John, 70, 81, 105n, 142; doctrines, 87–93
Mirabeau, Victor Riqueti, Marquis de, 94–96
Mises, Ludwig von, 128
Molière, Jean Baptiste Poquelin, 12
money: love of, as interest, 54–57; lust for, as sin, 9–10, 12, 20–21, 41. See also wealth

money-making: as calm passion, 63–66; as harmless pursuit, 56–63, 134; nineteenth-century ideas on, 125; and Protestant ethic, 129–30

Montesquieu, Charles Louis de Secondat, Baron de, 9, 55, 56, 70, 93, 99, 119, 125, 127, 136; on bills of exchange, 72–74, 76–78; on commerce, 70–80; on *doux commerce*, 60; and Physiocrats, 96–97; on power, 77–78; on property, 74, 94; Smith compared with, 102, 104, 107; Steuart influenced by, 81–82, 85–88

Montesquieu-Steuart doctrines, 113, 117–18, 120, 123, 124, 128

Morelly, 57

Napoleonic Wars, 113
nations, "polished" and "rude or barbarous," 61, 119–20
nature, state of, 53
Nedham, Marchamont, 36n
Nef, John U., 144
Nicole, Pierre, 16–17n

Oresmus, Nicolas, 141

Pascal, Blaise, 11, 12, 16
passions: and aristocracy, 112; countervailing, 20–31, 41, 78; and economic expansion, 125–26; inconstancy of, 52–53; and interest, dichotomy of, 42–48, 58, 63–64, 69–70, 73, 102, 125; interest and interests as tamers of, 31–42; and interests as synonyms, 110–11; and reason, 43–44; Smith's attitude toward, 108, 110–11; three basic, 9–10, 12,

20–21; transformed into virtues, 16–18; and war, 79

personality, effect of capitalism on, 132, 133

Peters, Richard S., 137

Physiocrats, 70, 104, 122; economic expansion, views of, 93–96; political organization, views of, 96–99

Plato, 43

Pocock, J. G. A., vii–viii, 40n, 57n, 143, 144

Polanyi, Michael, 69

political organization, Physiocrats' views on, 96–99

power: countervailing, 77–78; lust for, as sin, 9–10, 12

power, restrictions on: Millar's ideas, 89–93; Montesquieu's ideas, 77–78, 87–88; Proudhon's ideas, 128; Steuart's ideas, 82–88

powers, separation of, 77–78

praise, desire for, 10

property: Montesquieu's view of, 74, 94; movable and fixed, 73–76, 94; private, arguments for, 127–28; Spinoza's view of, 74–75

Protestant ethic, 129–30

Proudhon, Pierre Joseph, 128, 145

Prudentius, 21n

public debt, 75–76

Pufendorf, Samuel von, 53

Quesnay, François, 75, 94–96, 98, 103

Raab, Felix, 36n, 37n, 139

Racine, Jean Baptiste, 11

reason, interest, and passions, 43–44, 46, 74n

INDEX

Renaissance, pursuit of honor
and glory in, 11
ressentiment, 121, 126
Retz, Jean François de Gondi,
Cardinal de, 45–46, 135
revolution of 1848, 124
riots and rebellions, Millar's
view of, 89–93
Robertson, William, 61, 83
Rohan, Henri, Duc de, 34, 36–
37, 42, 51, 111
Romanticism, 132
Rosenberg, Nathan, 18n, 143,
144
Rousseau, Jean Jacques, 14,
27–28, 107; on *amour de soi*
and *amour propre*, 109; on
interests and passions, 126
Rudé, George, 92, 142

Sacy, Louis de, 141
Samuelson, Paul A., 119n
Santayana, George, 133
Savary, Jacques, 59–60, 62n,
140
Schiller, Johann Christoph
Friedrich von, 48
Scholastics, 9
Schumpeter, Joseph A., 101n,
134–35, 136
Scotland, moral philosophy in,
64, 70
Scottish Enlightenment, 70, 81,
88, 119
self-interest, *see* interest
Sen, S. R., 141
separation of powers, 77–78
Shackleton, Robert, 77n
Shaftesbury, Anthony Ashley
Cooper, Lord, 37, 46, 47, 139;
on money-making, 64–65
Shklar, Judith, viii
Silhon, Jean de, 39, 138
Simmel, Georg, 55–56

sin: Augustine's idea of, 9–10;
avarice as, 12, 20–21, 41
Skinner, A. S., 142
Skinner, Quentin, viii, 57n
Smith, Adam, 18–19, 39–40,
64n, 66, 69, 70, 75, 81, 88,
119, 120, 130, 138, 143; doctrines 100–12; economic expansion, view of, 93–94, 96,
100–12; *Theory of Moral
Sentiments* and *Wealth of
Nations* compared, 108–10
Smith, D. W., 17n, 138
social contract, 53
socialism, 127
Sombart, Werner, 136
South Sea Bubble, 57
Spain, aristocratic ideal in, 58
Spinoza, Benedict, 13–14, 21,
44, 46, 52, 139, 141; on property, 74–75
state of nature, 53
Steuart, Sir James, 49–50, 70,
75, 93, 99, 139; on commerce,
81–83; doctrines, 81–87;
Montesquieu's influence on,
81–82, 85–88; and Physio-
crats, 94; Smith compared
with, 102, 104, 107. *See also*
Montesquieu-Steuart doc-
trines.
Stourzh, Gerald, 45n
Strauss, Leo, 13n, 137
sublimation, 17
Sutcliffe, F. E., 138

Tendler, Judith, viii
Thatcher, Sanford, viii
Thomas, Keith, 136–37, 144,
145
Thompson, E. P., 142
Tocqueville, Alexis de, 119,
122–25, 135
Tönnies, Ferdinand, 120

151

trade, *see* commerce

Ure, Andrew, 92

Vauvenargues, Luc de Clapiers,
Marquis de, 27, 57
Veblen, Thorstein, 144
Venturi, Franco, 137
Vermassung, 126
Vico, Giambattista, 14, 17, 19,
130, 137
Viner, Jacob, 37–38n, 60, 139,
140
virtues: battle against vices, 21;
passions transformed into,
16–18
Voltaire, François Marie
Arouet, 141

Walpole, Sir Robert, 57

Walzer, Michael, viii, 137
war: and capitalism, 134–35;
and commerce, 79, 80
watch, metaphor of, 85, 86–87,
93, 94, 122
wealth: fear of losing, 121, 125;
Ferguson's ideas on, 120–21,
125; and power, Smith's
doctrine of, 100–101; as
property, 94–96; pursuit of,
in Smith's doctrine, 108.
See also money
Weaver, Paul, 138
Weber, Max, 9, 129–30, 133,
136
Weulersse, Georges, 143
White, Lynn, 141
Wilkes riots, 92
Winch, Donald, viii

Library of Congress Cataloging in Publication Data

Hirschman, Albert O.
    The passions and the interests.

    Includes bibliographical references.
    1. Capitalism—History.   2. Intellectual life—
History.   I. Title.
HB501.H523   332'.041'09   76-24293
ISBN 0-691-04214-4
ISBN 0-691-00357-2 pbk.